AF479240

Movies

DISCOVERING CAREERS

Movies

Ferguson's

An Infobase Learning Company

Movies

Copyright © 2012 by Infobase Learning

All rights reserved. No part of this book may be reproduced or utilized in any form or by any means, electronic or mechanical, including photocopying, recording, or by any information storage or retrieval systems, without permission in writing from the publisher. For information contact:

Ferguson's
An imprint of Infobase Learning
132 West 31st Street
New York NY 10001

Library of Congress Cataloging-in-Publication Data

Movies.
   p. cm. — (Discovering careers)
 Includes bibliographical references and index.
 ISBN-13: 978-0-8160-8058-8 (hardcover : alk. paper)
 ISBN-10: 0-8160-8058-5 (hardcover : alk. paper) 1. Motion pictures—
Vocational guidance—Juvenile literature. 2. Motion picture industry—
Vocational guidance—Juvenile literature. I. Ferguson Publishing.
 PN1995.9.P75M58 2011
 791.43′0293—dc23
               2011023558

Ferguson's books are available at special discounts when purchased in bulk quantities for businesses, associations, institutions, or sales promotions. Please call our Special Sales Department in New York at (212) 967-8800 or (800) 322-8755.

You can find Ferguson's on the World Wide Web at
http://www.infobaselearning.com

Text design by Erik Lindstrom and Erika K. Arroyo
Cover design by Takeshi Takahashi and Alicia Post
Composition by Erik Lindsrom
Cover printed by Yurchak Printing, Landisville, Pa.
Book printed and bound by Yurchak Printing, Landisville, Pa.
Printed in the United States of America

This book is printed on acid-free paper.

CONTENTS

Introduction

You may not have decided yet what you want to be in the future. And you don't have to decide right away. You do know that right now you are interested in movies. Do any of the statements below describe you? If so, you may want to begin thinking about what a career in movies might mean for you.

___I enjoy performing in front of an audience.
___I like to make movies with my video camera.
___I enjoy putting on plays with my friends.
___I like to make or build things.
___I like to write songs, plays, or stories.
___I like to listen to or record sounds and music.
___I watch as many movies as I can.
___I play in the school band.
___I enjoy photography.
___I make my own clothes and jewelry.
___I spend a lot of time using art, illustration, or movie-editing programs on my computer.
___I enjoy drawing.
___I am fascinated by cartoons and the methods used to create them.
___I like to dance.
___I like to discover new music, movies, or books and tell my friends about them.
___I like to perform stunts with my bike.

Discovering Careers: Movies is a book about careers in movie-making, from actors to film directors to screenwriters. Careers in this field can be found on film sets, in recording studios, in business offices, in production houses, and in art studios. While the film industry is centered in Los Angeles and New York, workers are employed in most major cities in the United States and throughout the world.

This book describes many possibilities for future careers in moviemaking. Read through it and see how the different careers are connected. For example, if you are interested in working as a performer, you should read the Actors chapter, but also read about Dancers and Choreographers and Stunt Performers. If you are interested in working behind the scenes in a creative position, you will want to read about Cinematographers, Costume Designers, Film Directors, Production Designers and Art Directors, Screenwriters, and other careers. If your interests are more technical in nature, you will want to read about Lighting Technicians, and Special and Visual Effects Technicians, and other careers. Perhaps you want to write about the movies. If so, a career as a Movie Writer and Critic might be in your future. Go ahead and explore!

What Do Movie-Industry Workers Do?

The first section of each chapter begins with a heading such as "What Film Editors Do" or "What Talent Agents and Scouts Do." It tells what it's like to work at this job. It describes typical responsibilities and assignments. You will find out about working conditions. Which movie workers are employed on film sets? Which ones work at computers in offices? This section answers these and other questions.

How Do I Become a Movie-Industry Worker?

The section called "Education and Training" tells you what schooling you need for employment in each job—a high school diploma, training at a junior college, a college degree, or more. It also talks about on-the-job training that you can expect to receive after you're hired, and whether or not you must complete an apprenticeship program.

How Much Do Movie-Industry Workers Earn?

The "Earnings" section gives salary figures for the job described in the chapter. These figures give you a general idea of how much money people with this job can make. Keep in mind that many people really earn more or less than the amounts given here because actual salaries depend on many different things, such as the size of the company, the location of the company, and the amount of education, training, and experience you have. Generally, but not always, bigger companies located in major cities pay more than smaller ones in smaller cities and towns, and people with more education, training, and experience earn more. Also remember that these figures are current salaries. They will probably be different by the time you are ready to enter the workforce.

What Will the Future Be Like for Movie-Industry Workers?

The "Outlook" section discusses the employment outlook for the career: whether the total number of people employed in this career will increase or decrease in the coming years and whether jobs in this field will be easy or hard to find. These predictions are based on economic conditions, the size and makeup of the population, foreign competition, and new technology. They come from the U.S. Department of Labor, professional associations, and other sources.

Keep in mind that these predictions are general statements. No one knows for sure what the future will be like. Also remember that the employment outlook is a general statement about an industry and does not necessarily apply to everyone. A determined and talented person may be able to find a job in an industry or career with the worst outlook. And a person without ambition and the proper training will find it difficult to find a job in even a booming industry or career field.

Where Can I Find More Information?

Each chapter includes a sidebar called "For More Info." It lists resources that you can contact to find out more about the field and careers in the field. You will find names, addresses, phone numbers, e-mail addresses, and Web sites of movie-oriented associations and organizations.

Extras

Every chapter has a few extras. There are photos that show movie workers in action. There are sidebars and notes on ways to explore the field, fun facts, profiles of people in the field, and lists of Web sites and books that might be helpful. At the end of the book you will find three additional sections: "Glossary," "Browse and Learn More," and "Index." The Glossary gives brief definitions of words that relate to education, career training, or employment that you may be unfamiliar with. The Browse and Learn More section lists movie-related books, periodicals, and Web sites to explore. The Index includes all the job titles mentioned in the book.

It's not too soon to think about your future. We hope you discover several possible career choices in the movie industry. Happy hunting!

Actors

What Actors Do

Actors perform in movies, stage plays, and television, video, and radio productions. They use voice and gestures (movement of the limbs or body) to play, or portray, different characters. Actors spend a lot of time looking for available parts. They read and study the parts and then audition (try out) for the film's casting director, director, and producers. In film and television, actors must also do screen tests, which are scenes recorded on film. Casting directors, producers, and directors study these screen tests to decide if the actor is the right person for the role. Once selected for a role, actors memorize their lines and rehearse with other cast members. If the production includes singing and dancing, it requires more rehearsal time.

Film actors may spend weeks, months, and even up to a year on one production, which often takes place on location—that is, in different parts of the world. For example, a film may be shot in a desert, in a forest, in a big city, or on a film soundstage (a special building where movies are filmed). Film and television actors usually perform scenes out of sequence during filming—they may perform the last scene first, for example. They also may have to repeat the same scene many times.

Acting is often seen as a glamorous profession, yet many actors work long and irregular hours for both rehearsals and performances, often at low wages. Actors must frequently travel to work on location. This means that they are away from their family and friends for long periods of time.

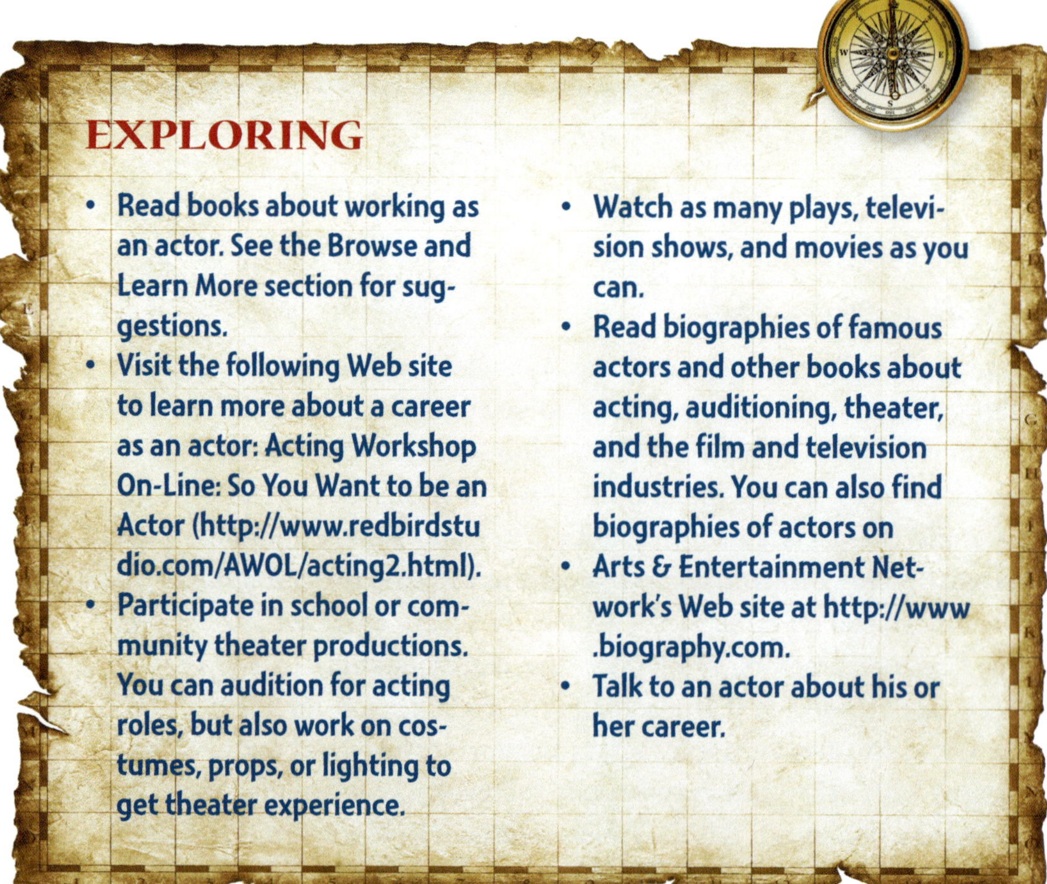

- Read books about working as an actor. See the Browse and Learn More section for suggestions.
- Visit the following Web site to learn more about a career as an actor: Acting Workshop On-Line: So You Want to be an Actor (http://www.redbirdstudio.com/AWOL/acting2.html).
- Participate in school or community theater productions. You can audition for acting roles, but also work on costumes, props, or lighting to get theater experience.
- Watch as many plays, television shows, and movies as you can.
- Read biographies of famous actors and other books about acting, auditioning, theater, and the film and television industries. You can also find biographies of actors on
- Arts & Entertainment Network's Web site at http://www.biography.com.
- Talk to an actor about his or her career.

Besides natural acting talent, actors need a good memory, a fine speaking voice, and, if possible, the ability to sing and dance. Actors who appear in musicals usually have studied singing and dancing for years in addition to their training in drama. Since it takes many years to break into the movie industry, they also must be determined and keep trying until they land their first acting job. They should also have a backup career in mind in case they never make it in Hollywood.

Education and Training

In high school, take as many drama classes as possible and participate in theater productions. High school and community

An actress (left) discusses a scene with a director. (Jim Lavrakas, AP Photo/
The Anchorage Daily News)

theaters offer acting opportunities. Large cities such as New York, Chicago, and Los Angeles have public high schools for the performing arts. Special dramatic arts schools, located mainly in New York and Los Angeles, also offer training.

Although it is not required, a college education is helpful. Many aspiring actors complete at least a bachelor's degree in film, theater, or the dramatic arts. Some earn a master of fine arts degree. More than 150 programs in theater arts are accredited by the National Association of Schools of Theatre.

Fame & Fortune: Daniel Radcliffe

Daniel Radcliffe is many things—actor, poet, activist. However, he will forever be known to the world as his most famous character, the bespectacled wizard, Harry Potter.

Radcliffe got his start in the acting industry at a very young age when he convinced his mother, a casting agent, to send his picture to a British television network that was looking to cast an upcoming adaptation of *David Copperfield.* Radcliffe won the role, launching the start of his acting career.

Other roles followed, until he won the lead role in *Harry Potter and the Philosopher's Stone* at age 11. This movie was based on the wildly popular book written by J. K. Rowling. Radcliffe played Harry Potter in all seven movies that followed, telling the story of Harry Potter and his Hogwarts School friends as they undertook many adventures.

Today, Radcliffe is busy pursuing roles on the stage and screen, many of which showcase his maturing acting skills. He is also active in many humanitarian causes. He works to raise money for sick children, victims of natural disasters, and others causes.

Radcliffe's portrait was recently displayed in Britain's National Portrait Gallery, earning him the distinction of being the youngest nonroyal to be included.

Sources: Answers.com,
Danradcliffe.com

Earnings

According to the U.S. Department of Labor, the mean yearly salary for movie actors was $89,772 in 2010. Some actors just starting out make no or little annual salary until they land acting roles. Many have to work at other jobs (such as waiter or office clerk) in order to earn enough money to pay their bills.

In all areas of acting, well-known performers have salary rates above the minimums, and the salaries of the few top stars are many times higher. In film, top stars may earn as much as $20 million per film, and, after receiving a percentage of the gross (the total earnings) earned by the film, these stars can earn far, far more.

Movie actors may also receive additional payments known as residuals as part of their guaranteed salary. A residual is a payment that is given to the actor whenever films in which they appear are rerun, licensed for TV exhibition, or released on DVD or online. Residuals often exceed the actors' original salary and account for about one-third of all actors' income.

Outlook

There will be strong competition for acting jobs during the next decade. Many people want to become actors—especially in the film industry. In addition to the film industry, there are also opportunities in television and theater. In the last two decades, the field has grown considerably outside New York because many major cities have started their own professional theater companies. The number of dinner theaters and summer stock

Study with the Masters

- For more than 60 years, The Actors Studio has taught the "method" style of acting to some of the greatest actors. Method acting was developed from the work of Konstantin Stanislavsky of Russia, and was taught by Lee Strasberg. It was made famous by the actors Marlon Brando, Dustin Hoffman, Robert DeNiro, and many others.

- The Actors Studio now has a master of fine arts degree program at the New School for Drama in New York. The three-year program was created by studio members James Lipton, Paul Newman, Ellen Burstyn, Arthur Penn, Norman Mailer, Carlin Glynn, Lee Grant, and Peter Masterson.
- Visit http://www.theactorsstudio.org for more information about The Actors Studio.

FOR MORE INFO

The following is a professional union for actors in theater and "live" industrial productions:

Actors' Equity Association
165 West 46th Street
New York, NY 10036-2500
212-869-8530
http://www.actorsequity.org

This union represents television and radio performers, including actors, announcers, dancers, disc jockeys, newspersons, singers, specialty acts, sportscasters, and stuntpersons.

American Federation of Television and Radio Artists
260 Madison Avenue
New York, NY 10016-2401
212-532-0800
http://www.aftra.com

For answers to a number of frequently asked questions concerning drama education, visit the NAST Web site.

National Association of Schools of Theatre (NAST)
11250 Roger Bacon Drive, Suite 21
Reston, VA 20190-5248
703-437-0700
info@arts-accredit.org
http://nast.arts-accredit.org

This union represents film and television performers. It has general information on actors, directors, and producers.

Screen Actors Guild
5757 Wilshire Boulevard, 7th Floor
Los Angeles, CA 90036-3600
323-954-1600
http://www.sag.com

companies has also increased. Cable television programming continues to add new acting opportunities, but there always will be many more actors than there are roles to play. Many actors also work as secretaries, waiters, taxi drivers, or in other jobs to earn extra income.

Animators

What Animators Do

Animators design the cartoons you see at the movies, on television, and on the Internet. They also create the digital effects for many films and commercials. Making a big animated film, such as *Up, Finding Nemo,* or *WALL-E* requires a team of many creative people. Each animator on the team works on one small part of the film. On a small production, animators may be involved in many different parts of the project's development.

An animated film begins with a script. *Screenwriters* plan the story line, or plot, and write it with dialogue and narration. *Designers* read the script and decide how the film should look—should it be set in the future, the past, or in today's times. Should it be funny or serious or a combination of both? They then draw some of the characters and backgrounds. These designs are then passed on to a *storyboard artist* who illustrates the whole film in a series of frames, similar to a very long comic strip. Based on this storyboard, an artist can then create a detailed layout.

In the past, cell animation was the most common form of animation. It is still used today by some animators. *Cell animators* examine the script, the storyboard, and the layout, and begin to prepare the finished artwork frame by frame, or cell by cell, on a combination of paper and transparent plastic sheets. Some animators create the "key" drawings. These are the drawings that capture the characters' main expressions (smiling,

EXPLORING

- Read books about a career as an animator. See the Browse and Learn More section for suggestions.
- Visit Cartoonster (http://www .kidzdom.com/tutorials) to learn how to make your own animations.
- View as many animated films, television shows, and Internet shorts that you can to learn about different types of animation styles.
- Practice sketching. Carry a sketchpad around in order to quickly capture images and gestures that seem interesting to you.

- There are many computer animation software programs available that teach basic principles and techniques. Use these to hone your skills.
- Participate in school or community art clubs. Draw posters to publicize activities, such as sporting events, dances, and meetings.
- Some video cameras have stop-motion buttons that allow you to take a series of still shots. You can use this feature to experiment with claymation and other stop-motion techniques.
- Talk to an animator about his or career.

frowning, etc.) and gestures (pointing, clapping, etc.) at important parts in the plot. Other animators create the "in between" drawings—the drawings that fill in the spaces between one key drawing and the next. The cells are painted by hand or scanned into a computer. With computer programs, animators add color, special effects, and other details.

Another type of animation is stop-motion animation. In this type of animation, an object, such as a clay creature or doll, is photographed, moved slightly, and photographed again. The process is repeated hundreds of thousands of times. Movies,

An animator works with the characters for Tim Burton's stop-motion animated film, Corpse Bride (TopFoto/The Image Works)

such as *The Nightmare Before Christmas, Chicken Run,* and *James and the Giant Peach,* were animated this way.

The most popular type of animation today is created by using a computer. In computer-generated animation (also known as digital animation), the animator creates all the images directly on the computer screen. Computer programs can create effects like shadows, reflections, distortions, and dissolves. Computers are used to color animation art, whereas formerly, every frame was painted by hand. Computers also help animators create special effects and even entire films. One animation

Words to Learn

animatic a kind of digital story-board that allows animations to be viewed on a video monitor

CGI acronym for "computer-generated imagery," which refers to any artwork or animation created with computers

claymation one of the most common forms of stop-motion animation in which the objects being photographed are made of clay

computer animation the creation of moving images through the use of computers; also known as digital animation

dialogue the conversations between characters in a movie, television show, or book; dialogue advances the plot or tells the audience important facts about each character's personality, actions, or history

fps frames per second; in general, the higher the number of frames, the better the animation will be

kinematics animating a model to move the way a human moves

layers used in complex animation to help manipulate objects; different objects can be assigned different layers and then moved independently

modeling the process used to make animated objects from a real object; animators use models to help them envision the object and figure out how to draw its movements on flat paper

narration the voice-over in a film or television show that fills in the details of a story

rendering making a character or an inanimate object seem life-like; artists use color, shadow, texture, and light to render

stop-motion animation animation produced by arranging actual objects, taking a picture of them, repositioning the objects with slight differences, then taking another picture of them, and so on; the end result creates an illusion of motion when they are viewed in sequence

storyboard an outline of an animation in a series of drawings in multiple frames

Major Animation Studios

Blue Sky Studios
http://www.blueskystudios.com

DreamWorks Animation SKG
http://www.dreamworks
animation.com

Industrial Light & Magic
http://www.ilm.com

Rhythm & Hues Studios
http://www.rhythm.com

Sony Pictures Imageworks
http://www.sonypictures.com/
imageworks

program, Macromedia's Flash, has given rise to an entire Internet cartoon subculture.

Education and Training

Art and drawing classes will prepare you for a career in animation. Photography classes can help you to develop visual composition skills. English composition and literature classes will help you develop creative writing skills. Computer classes are extremely important for learning to use art-related software, such as illustration, graphics, and animation programs.

A college education isn't required, but many animators have at least a bachelor's degree in computer animation, digital art, graphic design, or art. There are many animation programs offered at universities and art institutes across the country. Additionally, aspiring animators should learn as many different software packages as possible, including Maya, PhotoShop, Final Cut, Premiere, and After Effects.

FOR MORE INFO

For information about animated films and digital effects, visit the AWN Web site, which includes feature articles, a list of schools, and a career section.

Animation World Network (AWN)
6525 Sunset Boulevard, Garden Suite 10
Hollywood, CA 90028-7212
323-606-4200
info@awn.com
http://www.awn.com

The guild represents the interests of animation professionals in California. Visit its Web site for information on training, earnings, and the animation industry.

Animators Guild Local 839
1105 North Hollywood Way
Burbank, CA 91505-2528
818-845-7500
info@animationguild.org
http://www.animationguild.org

For information on animation, contact
International Animated Film Society-ASIFA Hollywood
2114 West Burbank Boulevard
Burbank, CA 91506-1232
818-842-4691
info@asifa-hollywood.org
http://www.asifa-hollywood.org

For an art school directory, contact
National Art Education Association
1806 Robert Fulton Drive, Suite 300
Reston, VA 20191-4348
703-860-8000
info@arteducators.org
http://www.arteducators.org

Visit the society's Web site for information about festivals and presentations and news about the industry.

Visual Effects Society
5535 Balboa Boulevard, Suite 205
Encino, CA 91316-1544
818-981-7861
info@VisualEffectsSociety.com
http://www.visualeffectssociety.com

This nonprofit organization represents the professional interests of women (and men) in animation. Visit its Web site for industry information, links to animation blogs, details on membership for high school students, and its quarterly newsletter.

Women in Animation
wia@womeninanimation.org
http://wia.animationblogspot.com

Earnings

Multimedia artists and animators who work in the movie industry earned mean yearly salaries of $72,380 in 2010, according to the U.S. Department of Labor. Salaries for all animators ranged from less than $34,000 to more than $99,000.

Outlook

Opportunities in animation are expected to be good during the next decade. People of all ages love animated films. They make millions of dollars at the box office. Cable television is also producing more and more successful animated series for both children and adults. Animation is also being made for use in cell phones, MP3 players, tablet computers, and other types of mobile technology. It is also being used in scientific research and other settings outside the entertainment industry.

Many people want to become animators. As a result, it will be hard to land a job at a big animation studio. Those with advanced degrees and a lot of creativity will have the best chances of securing employment.

Cinematographers

What Cinematographers Do

Cinematographers run the cameras during the making of a film or video. They work closely with directors, actors, and other members of the film crew. Cinematographers work on feature films, educational films, industrial training films, documentaries, and commercials. They have different job duties based on the size of the production. For a documentary with a small crew, a cinematographer may set up the lighting and camera equipment. For a larger production, the cinematographer might focus solely on running the camera, while a team of assistants helps out with loading and unloading film and setting up the equipment.

Cinematographers begin work on a film project by reading the script. (A script is the written version of what happens in a film or television show.) They discuss with the director how to film each scene. They decide whether to film from across the room, or up close to the actors. They decide whether to use bright lighting with lots of shadows or more muted, even lighting. They decide on camera angles, how the camera moves, and how to frame each scene. Cinematographers also have a great deal of technical knowledge about film. This helps them decide which cameras, film, and filters to use. Cinematographers are also in charge of the film crew. They hire various assistants and tell them how to film each scene.

Cinematographers work both indoors and outdoors. They sometimes spend months on location away from home. Loca-

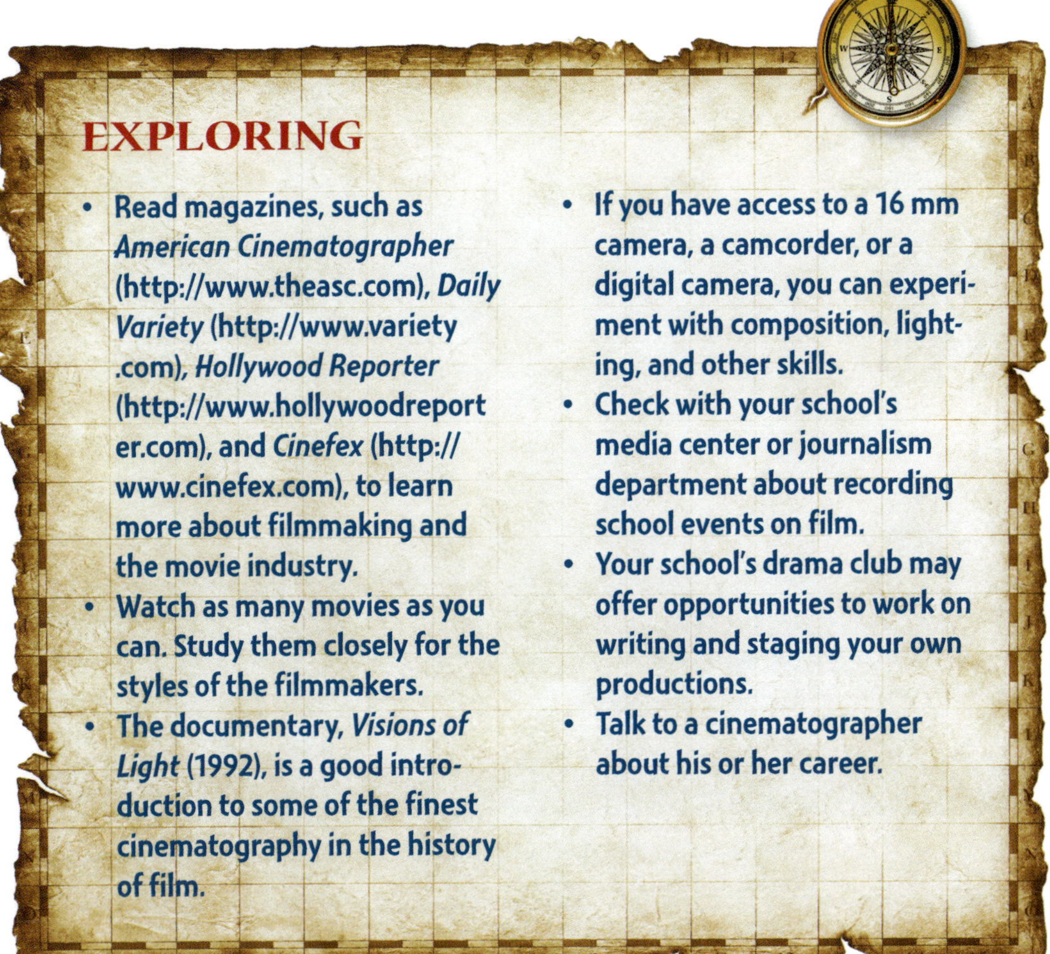

- Read magazines, such as *American Cinematographer* (http://www.theasc.com), *Daily Variety* (http://www.variety.com), *Hollywood Reporter* (http://www.hollywoodreporter.com), and *Cinefex* (http://www.cinefex.com), to learn more about filmmaking and the movie industry.
- Watch as many movies as you can. Study them closely for the styles of the filmmakers.
- The documentary, *Visions of Light* (1992), is a good introduction to some of the finest cinematography in the history of film.
- If you have access to a 16 mm camera, a camcorder, or a digital camera, you can experiment with composition, lighting, and other skills.
- Check with your school's media center or journalism department about recording school events on film.
- Your school's drama club may offer opportunities to work on writing and staging your own productions.
- Talk to a cinematographer about his or her career.

tions may range from a dusty desert, to a freezing mountaintop, to a busy, city street. When working on smaller productions, there may be a limited budget and a smaller film crew. In this instance, cinematographers may have to load and unload film from the camera, set up tripods (a three-legged object that holds up the camera), and carry the camera long distances. They participate in long hours of rehearsal before they actually start to film a scene. Although all their work is behind the scenes, cin-

A cinematographer (left) and a director shoot a sequence for a short film. (Jessica Griffin, AP Photo)

ematographers play an important part in the appearance and the success of the final film.

Cinematographers work for motion picture studios, production companies, independent producers, and documentary filmmakers. Some work on a freelance basis.

Education and Training

Art and photography courses can help you understand the basics of lighting and composition. When you get to high school, take broadcast journalism or media courses that teach camera operation and video production.

A college degree is not always necessary to find a position as a cinematographer. Experience and artistic talent is much more important. Many cinematographers, though, get that valuable experience during their college studies. Many colleges and art schools offer programs in film or cinematography. Your training should include all aspects of camera operations and lighting. It is important to practice working on a team. You must be able to give directions as well as follow them.

Earnings

When starting out, apprentice filmmakers may make no money. They may even spend their own money to pay for, or finance, their own projects. Since they usually are hired one film at a time, there may be periods of unpaid time between assignments. As they gain experience, they will begin to find more jobs and earn more. According to the U.S. Department of Labor, camera operators (a category that includes cinematographers) in the movie industry earned an average salary of $52,380 a year in 2010. Salaries for all camera operators ranged from less than $21,000 to $81,000 or more. Experienced cinematographers working on big-budget Hollywood productions can make more than $1 million a year, but very few cinematographers earn that much.

Award Winners

Following are recent Oscar winners for cinematography:

- 2010: Wally Pfister, *Inception*
- 2009: Mauro Fiore, *Avatar*
- 2008: Anthony Dod Mantle, *Slumdog Millionaire*
- 2007: Robert Elswit, *There Will Be Blood*
- 2006: Guillermo Navarro, *Pan's Labyrinth*
- 2005: Dion Beebe, *Memoirs of a Geisha*
- 2004: Robert Richardson, *The Aviator*
- 2003: Russell Boyd, *Master and Commander: The Far Side of the World*
- 2002: Conrad L. Hall, *Road to Perdition*
- 2001: Andrew Lesnie, *The Lord of the Rings: The Fellowship of the Ring*
- 2000: Peter Pau, *Crouching Tiger, Hidden Dragon*

For more information on Academy Award-winning cinematographers, visit http://www.oscars.org/awardsdatabase.

Outlook

Many people want to work in the movie industry. This means that there are far more qualified cinematographers than there are job openings. If you are skilled and well trained, you should find positions, but it could take a long time before you find work in industry hotspots such as Los Angeles or New York.

You may find better opportunities working on TV commercials, documentaries, or educational films. Cinematographers will find some new opportunities helping to make made-for-Internet broadcasts, such as digital movies, sports features, music videos, and general entertainment programs. Cinematog-

FOR MORE INFO

For a variety of movie-related resources, visit the AFI Web site.

American Film Institute (AFI)
2021 North Western Avenue
Los Angeles, CA 90027-1657
323-856-7600
information@afi.com
http://www.afi.com

The ASC Web site has articles from *American Cinematographer* magazine, industry news, and a tips and tricks for cinematographers section.

American Society of Cinematographers (ASC)
PO Box 2230
Hollywood, CA 90078-2230
800-448-0145
http://www.theasc.com

For information on union membership, contact

International Cinematographers Guild (IATSE Local 600)
National Office/Western Region
7755 Sunset Boulevard
Hollywood, CA 90046-3911
323-876-0160
https://www.cameraguild.com

raphers of the future will be working more closely with visual effects experts. Computer technology can create crowd scenes, underwater images, and other effects more easily and cheaply. Cinematographers will have to approach a film with an understanding of which shots can be made digitally and which will need traditional methods of filmmaking.

What Composers Do

Who wrote the exciting music you hear during movies such as *Harry Potter and the Goblet of Fire, Star Wars,* or *Toy Story*? *Composers* did, that's who. Composers write original scores and thematic music for films. A score is the music that plays throughout the film apart from any songs that may also be in the film. Composers write scores and music for movies, musical stage shows, television shows, radio and television, commercials, ballet and opera companies, orchestras, pop and rock bands, jazz combos, and other musical performing groups. Composers work in many different ways. Often they begin with a musical idea and write it down using standard music notation on paper or using a computer software program. They use their music training and their own personal sense of melody, harmony, rhythm, and structure. Some compose music as they play an instrument and may or may not write it down.

Most composers specialize in one style of music, such as classical, jazz, country, rock, or blues. Some combine several styles. Composers who work on commission (payment for a single work or a series of works) or on assignment meet with their clients to discuss the composition's theme, length, style, and the number and types of performers. Composers work at home, in offices, or in music studios. Some need to work alone to plan and build their musical ideas and others work with fellow musicians. Composing can take many long hours of work, and composing jobs may be irregular and low paying. However,

EXPLORING

- Read books about composing music for movies and the film industry in general. See the Browse and Learn More section for suggestions.
- Participate in musical programs offered by local schools, YMCA/YWCAs, and community centers.
- Learn to play a musical instrument, such as the piano, guitar, violin, or cello.
- Watch movies and listen to their musical scores.
- Attend concerts and recitals.
- Read about composers and their careers.
- Form or join a musical group and try to write music for your group to perform.
- Talk to a movie composer about his or her career.

composers take great pride in hearing their music performed, and successful commercial music composers can earn a lot of money. After the piece is completed, the composer usually attends rehearsals (practices) and works with the performers. The composer may have to revise parts of the piece until the client and the composer are satisfied.

Many composers never perform their own works, but others, especially pop, rock, jazz, country, or blues performers, compose music for their own bands to play.

To be a successful movie composer, you need artistic talent and creativity. You should also know a lot about various musical styles, the film industry, and the process of composing a musical work for film. Other important traits for composers include the ability to follow instructions, a willingness to receive

Film composer Ennio Morricone conducts the Budapest Symphonic Orchestra, performing his most popular film themes. (Boris Grdanoski, AP Photo)

constructive criticism, strong communication skills, and the ability to play at least one instrument.

Education and Training

Take as many music classes as possible—especially those that teach music composition. Participation in school choirs and music groups are also good ways to gain experience in the field.

All composers need to have a good ear and be able to notate, or write down, their music. Composers of musicals, symphonies, and other large works must have years of study in a college, conservatory, or other school of music. Composers of popular songs may not need as much training. However, studying music helps you develop and express your musical ideas better. Music school courses for those who wish to be composers include music theory, musical form, music history, composition, conducting, and arranging. Composers also play at least one musical instrument, usually piano, and some play several instruments.

Some colleges offer concentrations or certificates in film and television scoring. Once such program is the Scoring for Motion Pictures and Television Program at the University of Southern California. Visit http://www.usc.edu/schools/music/programs/smptv for more information on this interesting program.

Earnings

Most composers earn very little and work only part time. A few earn a great deal of money. Some composers work on commission. When a piece of music is commissioned, the composer receives a lump sum for writing it. Other composers work under contract with a music publishing, recording, or movie company. Their compositions become the property of the company. Some composers receive royalties, or payments for each performance or sale of the piece.

Where Composers Work

Most composers are self-employed. They are hired by the following employers to create musical compositions:

- advertising agencies
- colleges and universities
- dance companies
- film and television production companies
- musical artists
- musical theater producers
- music publishers
- record companies

The Greatest Film Scores of All Time

- *Gone With the Wind* (1939, Max Steiner)
- *Laura* (1944, David Raksin)
- *High Noon* (1952, Dimitri Tiomkin)
- *The Magnificent Seven* (1960, Elmer Bernstein)
- *Psycho* (1960, Bernard Herrmann)
- *Lawrence of Arabia* (1962, Maurice Jarre)
- *The Godfather* (1972, Nino Rota)
- *Chinatown* (1974, Jerry Goldsmith)
- *Jaws* (1975, John Williams)
- *Star Wars* (1977, composed by John Williams)

Source: American Film Institute

A major film studio may pay a composer $50,000 to $200,000 or more for a musical score. Salaries for all composers ranged from less than $22,000 to $85,000 or more in 2010, according to the U.S. Department of Labor.

Outlook

Strong job competition is expected for composers—especially in the movie industry. Only a small number of composers create music for movies, and many people want to enter the field. Despite this prediction, there will continue to be opportunities for composers. As long as there are movies, commercials, musicals, operas, and orchestras, and other musical performances, there will be a need for composers to write music.

FOR MORE INFO

For profiles of composers of concert music, visit the ACA Web site.

American Composers Alliance (ACA)
802 West 190th Street, 1st Floor
New York, NY 10040-3937
212-925-0458
info@composers.com
http://composers.com

For educational resources, contact
American Composers Forum
332 Minnesota Street, Suite East 145
St. Paul, MN 55101-1300
651-228-1407
http://www.composersforum.org

For career information, contact
American Federation of Musicians of the United States and Canada
1501 Broadway, Suite 600
New York, NY 10036-5505
212-869-1330
http://www.afm.org

For articles on songwriting and practical information about the business of music, contact
American Society of Composers, Authors, and Publishers
One Lincoln Plaza
New York, NY 10023-7129
212-621-6000
http://www.ascap.com

Visit the society's Web site for career resources, an online hall of fame, and information on *The SCORE*, its quarterly publication.

Society of Composers & Lyricists
8447 Wilshire Boulevard, Suite 401
Beverly Hills CA 90211-3209
310-281-2812
http://www.thescl.com

Costume Designers

What Costume Designers Do

Costume designers create the costumes seen in movies, in the theater, and on television. They also design costumes for figure skaters, ballroom dancers, and other performers. During the planning of a movie, costume designers read the script. They meet with directors and/or production designers to decide what types of costumes each character should wear for each scene.

Stories that take place in the past, called period pieces, require costume designers to know a lot about what people wore during different historical time periods in different parts of the world. For example, a costume designer may be asked to create costumes for a movie set in the Wild West of the 1800s, Egypt during the time of King Tut, or ancient Rome. Designers do research at libraries, museums, and universities to study the garments, shoes, hats, belts, bags, and jewelry worn by men, women, and children. They look at the colors and types of fabric used and how garments were made. Even for films that take place in modern times or in the future, costume designers might use ideas that come from looking at the details of historical fashions.

Once they complete their research, designers begin to make sketches of their costume ideas. They try to design each outfit to look authentic, or true to the time period when the story occurs. Designers also pay attention to the social status of each character, the season and weather for each scene, and the costumes of other characters in each scene. Many costume

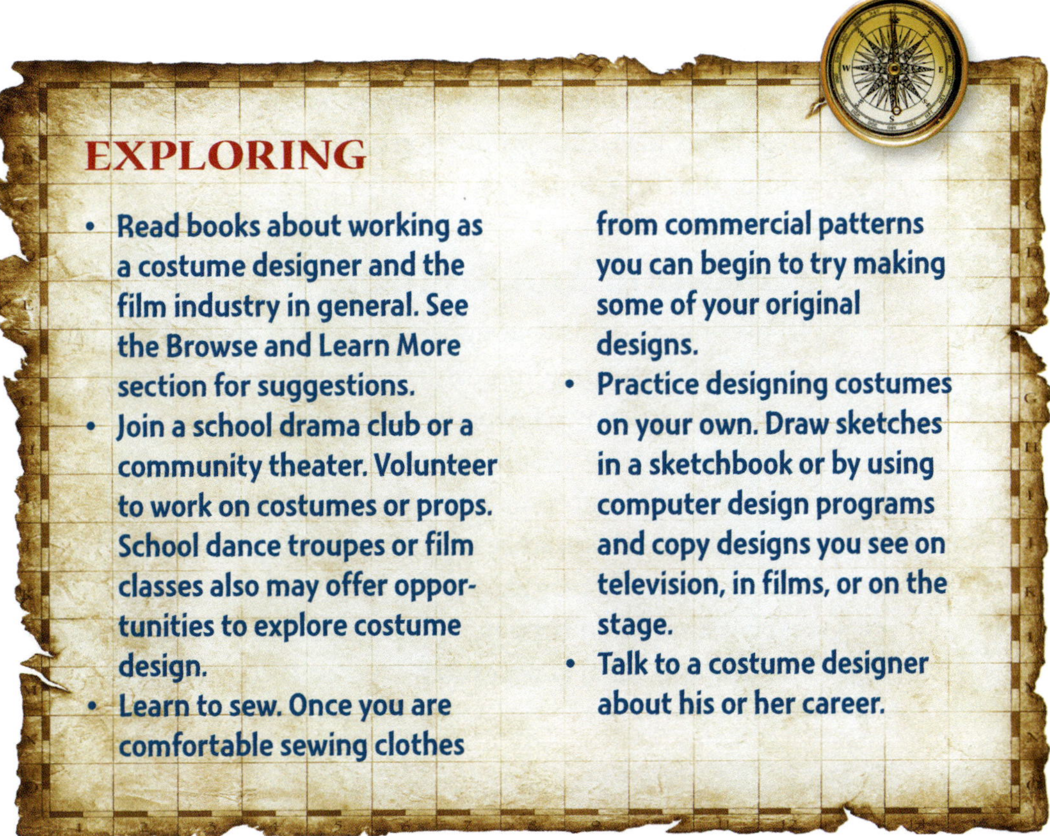

- Read books about working as a costume designer and the film industry in general. See the Browse and Learn More section for suggestions.
- Join a school drama club or a community theater. Volunteer to work on costumes or props. School dance troupes or film classes also may offer opportunities to explore costume design.
- Learn to sew. Once you are comfortable sewing clothes from commercial patterns you can begin to try making some of your original designs.
- Practice designing costumes on your own. Draw sketches in a sketchbook or by using computer design programs and copy designs you see on television, in films, or on the stage.
- Talk to a costume designer about his or her career.

designers now use computer-aided design programs to create design sketches.

Costume designers meet with directors and production designers for design approval. They also meet with stage designers, production designers, and art directors to be certain that the furniture and backdrops do not clash with the costumes. They meet with lighting designers to make sure that the lighting will not change the appearance of costume colors.

Costume designers decide whether to rent, purchase, or sew the costumes. They shop for clothing and accessories, fabrics, and sewing supplies. They also supervise assistants who do the sewing.

Costume designers work for production companies that create works for stage, television, and movies. Most job opportunities are found in New York and Los Angeles, although most large cities have film production and community theater companies that hire designers.

Education and Training

To become a costume designer, you need a high school diploma and a college degree in costume design, fashion design, or fiber art. You also need experience working in theater or film. In high school, take classes in art, theater, family and consumer science, math, and computer-aided design.

English and literature courses will help you read and understand scripts. History classes are helpful for researching historical costumes and time periods. Courses in sewing, designing, and draping are also necessary.

DID YOU KNOW?

Costumes include a lot more than clothing. Designers have to also consider accessories, such as the following:

- belts and girdles, including sword belts, sashes, and suspenders
- neckwear, such as ruffs, collars, cravats, neckties, and tie clasps
- eyeglasses, including monocles, lorgnettes, and pince nez
- fans
- gloves
- jewelry, including earrings, pins, necklaces, beads, bracelets, rings, and watches
- purses and pouches
- shawls
- umbrellas and parasols
- walking sticks and canes

Earnings

For feature films and television, costume designers earn daily rates for an eight-hour day or a weekly rate for an unlimited number of hours. Costume designers who work on television and theatrical films earned about $2,831 a week in 2010, according to rates established by the United Scenic Artists union, which sets minimum rates for its members. Assistant costume designers earned about $353 a day. Designers sometimes earn royalties on their designs. A royalty is paid if the design is used again by a film company or other organization.

Most costume designers work freelance and are paid per costume or show. Costume designers can charge between $90 and $500 per costume, but some costumes, such as those for figure skaters, can cost thousands of dollars.

Tips for Success

To be a successful costume designer, you should

- be very creative
- have good sewing, draping, and patterning skills
- be able to work well with others and follow directions
- be a good problem-solver
- be able to accept constructive criticism about your work
- have good design skills
- be able to work under deadline pressure

Outlook

Competition among costume designers is stiff and will remain so through the next decade. There are many more qualified costume designers than there are jobs. It will be hard to land a job as a costume designer for a major Hollywood movie project. There will be more opportunities in cable television and with independent motion picture companies, which are grow-

FOR MORE INFO

This union represents costume designers in film and television. For information on the industry and to view costume sketches, visit its Web site.

Costume Designers Guild
11969 Ventura Boulevard, 1st Floor
Studio City, CA 91604-2630
818-752-2400
cdgia@costumedesignersguild.com
http://www.costumedesignersguild.com

For information on costume design, contact

Costume Society of America
390 Amwell Road, Suite 402
Hillsborough, NJ 08844-1247
800-272-9447
national.office@costumesocietyamerica.com
http://www.costumesocietyamerica.com

For industry information, contact

National Costumers Association
121 North Bosart Avenue
Indianapolis, IN 46201-3729
317-351-1940
office@costumers.org
http://www.costumers.org

This union represents costume designers and other design professionals. For information on apprenticeship programs and other resources, contact

United Scenic Artists Local USA 829
29 West 38th Street, 15th Floor
New York, NY 10018-5504
212-581-0300
http://www.usa829.org

ing rapidly and will continue to expand in the next decade. New York City and Hollywood (Los Angeles) are the main centers for costume designers.

Dancers and Choreographers

What Dancers and Choreographers Do

Dancers and *choreographers* have played an important role in movies ever since the early days of Hollywood. Dancers use body movements to tell a story, express an idea or feeling, or entertain their audiences. Most dancers study some ballet or classical dance. Classical dance training gives dancers a good foundation for most other types of dance. Many of the standard dance terms used in all types of dance are the same terms used in 17th-century ballet.

Modern dance developed early in the 20th century as a departure from classical ballet. Early modern dancers danced barefoot and began to explore movement and physical expression in new ways. Jazz dance is a form of modern dance often seen in Broadway productions. Tap dance combines sound and movement as dancers tap out rhythms with metal cleats attached to the toes and heels of their shoes. Other dance forms include ballroom dance, folk or ethnic dance, and acrobatic dance.

Dancers who create new ballets or dance routines are called choreographers. Choreographers have a very good understanding of dance and music, as well as costume, lighting, and dramatics. Besides inventing new dance routines, choreographers teach their dances to performers and sometimes they direct and stage the presentation of their dances in movies and in theatrical productions.

EXPLORING

- Learn about famous movie dancers such as Cyd Charisse, Fred Astaire, Gene Kelly, Sammy Davis Jr., and Gregory Hines on the Internet and in books.
- Visit http://www.ket.org/artstoolkit/dance/glossary.htm for a glossary of dance-related terms.
- Take as many dance classes as you can. Try different types of dance.
- There are many instructional videos available that teach you ballet, tap, and ballroom dancing. It is best, though, to study with a teacher who can watch you and help you do the movements correctly, so you don't develop bad habits or injure yourself.
- Once you have learned some dance technique, begin to give recitals and performances.
- Audition for school or community stage productions that have dance numbers.
- Try to choreograph a dance routine for a school performance or community event.
- Watch as many famous dance-oriented movies (*Singin' in the Rain, 42nd Street, A Chorus Line, Staying Alive, Footloose, Chicago,* or *Billy Elliot*) as you can. Note what you like and dislike about the styles of dance and choreography.
- Talk to a dancer or choreographer about his or her career.

Choreographers know how to use movement and music to tell a story, create a mood, express an idea, or celebrate movement itself. Since dance is so closely related to music, choreographers must know about various musical styles and rhythms. They often hear a piece of music first and then choreograph a dance to it. Sometimes choreographers plan the dance, then choose the dancers and teach them movements. But most often they work with their dancers, and change the choreography to take best advantage of the dancers' abilities. Choreographers must also be flexible enough to change their dances to fit different performance spaces.

Education and Training

Choreographers almost always start their careers out as dancers. Dancers usually begin training around the age of 10. Some even begin as early as age seven or eight. They may study with private teachers or in ballet schools. Dancers who show promise in their early teens may receive professional training in a regional ballet school or a major ballet company. By the age of 17 or 18, dancers begin to audition for positions in professional dance companies.

Profile: Twyla Tharp (1941–   )

Dancer and choreographer Twyla Tharp is known for her imaginative works that combine modern and traditional dance movements. *Eight Jelly Rolls*, *Push Comes to Shove*, and *Bach Partita* are some of her works.

Tharp was born in Portland, Indiana, and studied music and dance as a child. While attending Barnard College in New York City, she studied dance with famous dancers and choreographers such as Merce Cunningham, Martha Graham, and others. Tharp first danced professionally with the Paul Taylor Dance Company. She formed her own company, Twyla Tharp Dance, in 1965 and also choreographed dances for the Joffrey Ballet, American Ballet Theatre, The Martha Graham Dance Company, and other dance companies. She choreographed the motion pictures *Hair* (1979), *Amadeus* (1984), and *White Nights* (1985), among other movies. She directed and choreographed the Broadway musical *Singin' in the Rain*. According to her Web site, Tharp has "choreographed more than 135 dances, five Hollywood movies, and directed and choreographed four Broadway shows." Visit http://www.twylatharp.org to learn more about her career.

Source: TwylaTharp.com

DID YOU KNOW?

Where Dancers and Choreographers Work

In addition to working in the movie industry, dancers and choreographers work for the following employers:

- dance companies
- local park districts
- opera companies
- schools
- self-employment
- senior citizens homes
- social service agencies
- television production companies
- theater companies
- video companies
- youth centers

Many colleges and universities offer degrees in dance with choreography classes. Although you do not need a college degree to become a dancer or choreographer, it can be helpful. Those who teach dance in a college or university often are required to have a degree.

Earnings

The U.S. Department of Labor reports that the median salary for dancers was $27,372 in 2010. Salaries ranged from less than $17,000 to $63,000 or more. That same year, choreographers earned a median salary of $37,660. The lowest paid 10 percent made $19,000 or less, while the highest paid 10 percent earned $71,000 or more.

Because of the lack of steady, well-paying work, many dancers and choreographers must make extra money by working at a second job. Some other job options include teaching dance, working several part-time dance jobs, or going outside the field for other work.

FOR MORE INFO

For information on all aspects of dance, contact

American Dance Guild
240 West 14th Street
New York, NY 10011-7218
http://americandanceguild.org

For articles and press releases about dance-related topics, visit the Dance/USA Web site.

Dance/USA
1111 16th Street, NW, Suite 300
Washington, DC 20036-4830
202-833-1717
http://www.danceusa.org

A directory of accredited programs is available from the NASD. Approved member institutions can also be found listed on its Web site, which also contains a helpful FAQ section for students.

National Association of Schools of Dance (NASD)
11250 Roger Beacon Drive, Suite 21
Reston, VA 20190-5248
703-437-0700
info@arts-accredit.org
http://nasd.arts-accredit.org/index.jsp

For information on careers in dance, contact

National Dance Association
American Alliance for Health, Physical Education, Recreation & Dance
1900 Association Drive
Reston, VA 20191-1598
800-213-7193, ext. 464
http://www.aahperd.org/nda

Outlook

It will be very difficult to land a job as a dancer or choreographer in the movie industry. There are many talented dancers and choreographers who are interested in working in the field—but only a small number of jobs. There will also be strong competition for jobs outside the movie industry. Very few dancers and choreographers work year round and they often take other jobs to make extra money. More than half the dance companies in the United States are in New York City, which means the majority of dancers and choreographers live there. There are opportunities in other large cities where there are dance companies and theater companies. There is some work available in television, too.

Film Directors

What Film Directors Do

Film directors coordinate the making of a movie. Most directors specialize in one type of film, such as documentaries (a nonfiction look at a topic such as poverty or a historical event), feature films, industrial films (training films made by corporations), and travelogues (nonfiction films about a particular country or region).

Directors work with actors, costume designers, cinematographers, screenwriters, lighting designers, production designers, producers, and many other workers. Directors are involved in every stage of making a movie—from hiring actors to helping edit the final film. They are also called *filmmakers* and *motion picture directors.*

While *producers* are in charge of the business and financial side of a film project, directors are in charge of the creative and technical sides. Usually a producer hires the director, but they work closely together. They plan a budget and production schedule, including time for research, casting (choosing actors), set design, filming, and editing.

Directors give instructions before, during, and after filming to many different people. They choose costumes, scenery, and music. During rehearsals, they plan the action carefully, telling actors how to move and interpret the script. They coach the actors to help them give their best performances. At the same time, directors give instructions for sets and lighting, and decide on the order and angles of camera shots. Once filming is

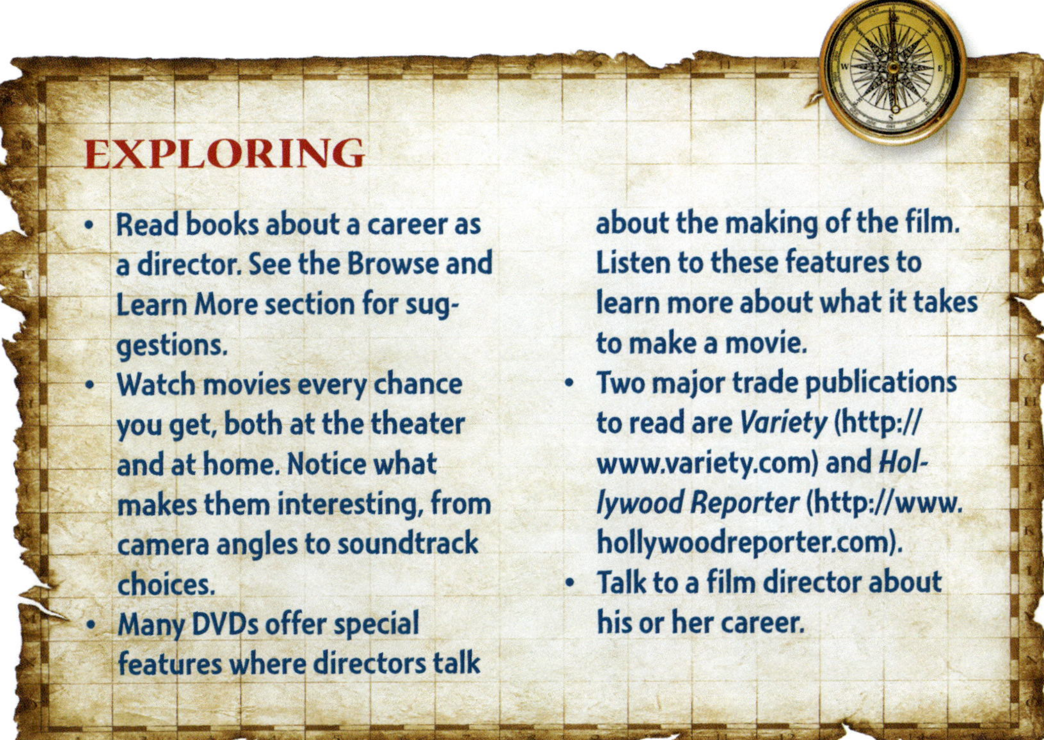

EXPLORING

- Read books about a career as a director. See the Browse and Learn More section for suggestions.
- Watch movies every chance you get, both at the theater and at home. Notice what makes them interesting, from camera angles to soundtrack choices.
- Many DVDs offer special features where directors talk about the making of the film. Listen to these features to learn more about what it takes to make a movie.
- Two major trade publications to read are *Variety* (http://www.variety.com) and *Hollywood Reporter* (http://www.hollywoodreporter.com).
- Talk to a film director about his or her career.

finished, they supervise film editing and provide suggestions on sound and special effects.

Most movie directors work on a freelance basis. They are hired by film studios (both major and independent), television stations, and cable networks. They also might develop their own independent projects. Outside of the movie industry, directors work for television studios, advertising agencies, corporations, record companies (music videos), and any other organization that needs a movie director. Some directors teach film studies at colleges and universities.

Directors of computer-generated animation manage animators and artists who create animated movies. They check that their work meets design standards and that the story is being told in an effective way. They also work with production design-

A director prepares for a scene. (Topham/The Image Works)

ers, art directors, and other production staff to make sure the project is manageable and meeting scheduling demands.

Education and Training

You can start now to prepare for a career in film directing. Take English literature classes to learn storytelling techniques. Theater classes will teach you about acting. Photography courses can teach you about visual composition. Your school may even offer film or video production classes. If so, take as many of these courses as possible.

Even though there are no specific requirements for becoming a film director, the most successful directors have a wide variety of talents and experience, as well as good business and management skills. You must be able to develop ideas, and be good at communicating with others.

Today, many film directors have degrees in film direction, film studies, cinematography, or related fields. There are many

Helping Hands: Steven Spielberg

In 1993, director Steven Spielberg made the Academy Award-winning film *Schindler's List,* a film about Oskar Schindler, a German man who saved the lives of more than 1,000 Jewish people during the Holocaust. The Holocaust is the name given to terrible events that occurred during World War II in which about 6 million people—many of them Jewish—were killed because of their ethnicity, religion, or for other reasons. Spielberg was deeply affected by the stories from the survivors of the Holocaust. He wanted these memories to survive, so future generations would know of the injustices of wartime. With this goal in mind, he established the Survivors of the Shoah Visual History Foundation.

Video testimonies from many Jewish survivors were collected, as well as from other groups who were persecuted. These groups included political prisoners, Gypsies, and those considered "unfit" or "unworthy" to live.

Since its founding in 1994, the foundation has archived more than 52,000 video testimonies, in 32 languages, representing more than 56 countries. In 2006, the foundation changed its name to the University of Southern California (USC) Shoah Foundation Institute for Visual History and Education after becoming part of USC's College of Letters, Arts and Sciences. Although its name has changed, its mission has not. With its archive of firsthand testimony, the foundation hopes to overcome prejudice, intolerance, and bigotry through scholarship, research, and education. It hopes to keep the stories of the Holocaust alive so that these horrible things never happen again.

Source: USC Shoah Foundation Institute

Tips for Success

To be a successful film director, you should

- be very creative
- be able to handle stress and meet deadlines
- have leadership skills
- be organized
- have good communication skills
- be willing to work long hours to meet production deadlines

colleges and universities that offer film majors with concentration in directing. These programs require you to direct your own films. They also offer internship and other practical learning experiences. The Directors Guild of America offers an Assistant Directors Training Program for those who have a bachelor's degree or two years of experience in movie production.

Many directors begin at small television stations or community theaters, or as production assistants for films. Many directors have worked for a number of years as actors, or in some other capacity within the industry, to gain experience.

Earnings

The median annual salary of film producers and directors was $109,860 in 2010, according to the U.S. Department of Labor. Among all directors, the lowest paid 10 percent earned less than $33,000, and the highest paid 10 percent earned more than $111,000.

Directors' salaries vary greatly. Most Hollywood film directors are members of the Directors Guild of America, and salaries (as well as hours of work and other employment conditions) are usually negotiated by this union. Keep in mind that because most directors are freelancers, they may have no income for many weeks out of the year.

FOR MORE INFO

For a variety of movie-related resources, visit the AFI Web site.

American Film Institute (AFI)
2021 North Western Avenue
Los Angeles, CA 90027-1657
323-856-7600
information@afi.com
http://www.afi.com

For information on a career as a director, contact
Directors Guild of America
7920 Sunset Boulevard
Los Angeles, CA 90046-3300
310-289-2000
http://www.dga.org

This is the trade association of the American film industry and home video and television industries. It operates the voluntary movie ratings system in cooperation with the National Association of Theater Owners.

Motion Picture Association of America
1600 Eye Street, NW
Washington, DC 20006-4010
202-293-1966
http://www.mpaa.org

Women in Film's mission is to "empower, promote, and mentor women in the entertainment and media industries." Visit its Web site for more information.

Women in Film
6100 Wilshire Boulevard, Suite 710
Los Angeles, CA 90048-5107
323-935-2211
info@wif.org
http://www.wif.org

Outlook

The number of movies being made is increasing as the cable television and video-rental industries continue to expand. Demand is also growing for directors to create movies and other content for viewing on portable electronic devices and on the Internet. Despite increasing interest in movies, many people are interested in becoming directors and there will be stiff competition for jobs. Directors with strong artistic ability and college training will have the best job prospects.

What Film Editors Do

Film editors perform an important role in the creation of movies and videos. They use special equipment and computer programs to alter unedited film, video, or digital files and arrange the material in order to create the most effective film possible. They work with producers and directors from the earliest phases of filming and production. In meetings with producers, editors learn about the goals of the film or video. The producer may explain the larger scope of the project so that the editor knows the best way to approach the work when it is time to edit the film. With the director, editors discuss the objective and story line of the movie or video. They may discuss scenes and camera angles before filming even begins so that the editor understands the director's vision of the final piece.

Once filming is complete, film editors rate and choose the segments that will be used. Sometimes there are five or 10 takes (different versions) of one scene. Editors select segments in terms of film or video quality, dramatic value, or other criteria. Editors refer to the script and the director's notes when making their choices. They time the film or video segments to specified lengths and reassemble the segments in a sequence so that they have the greatest effect and make the most sense. Editors and directors review the reassembled material on a video monitor, and editors make further adjustments and corrections until the final product is satisfactory to the director and producer.

EXPLORING

- Read books about working as an editor and the film industry. Here are two suggestions: *So You Want to Be a Film or TV Editor?*, by Amy Dunkleberger (Enslow Publishers, 2007) and *Movies*, by Annie Buckley (Cherry Lake Publishing, 2008).
- Join a film or video club at your school or community center.
- Research different kinds of film projects, including documentaries, short films, and feature films.
- Experiment with one of the many digital film-editing systems available for home computers. You can feed your own digital video into your computer, edit the material, and then add your own special effects and titles.
- Talk to a film editor about his or her career.

Film editors today are using nonlinear processes more often. In this process, the film is transferred to a digital format. Film editors use computer software programs such as Final Cut Pro or Adobe Premiere to track individual frames and edit the scenes. This information is stored on a computer hard drive and can be brought up instantly on a screen, allowing the editor to access and edit scenes and frames with the click of a mouse.

Sound editors work on film soundtracks. They often keep libraries of sounds that they frequently use for various projects, including natural sounds (such as thunder or raindrops), animal noises (such as the roar of a lion or the ribbit of a frog), motor sounds, or musical interludes. Some sound editors specialize in music, and others work with sound effects. They may

Tips for Success

To be a successful film editor, you should

- be creative
- have strong communication skills
- know a lot about film editing
- be able to work well with others
- have good computer skills
- be organized
- have good time-management skills
- be able to work under deadline-pressure
- be willing to continue to learn throughout your career

use unusual objects, machines, or computer-generated noisemakers to create a desired sound for a film.

Education and Training

In high school take courses in English, speech, theater, and other classes that will allow you to develop your creativity. Take computer classes to become comfortable using computer programs.

Training to work as a film editor takes many years. The best educational background is in the liberal arts. Some studios require a bachelor's degree for those seeking positions as editors. English, journalism, theater, or film are good majors to pursue. Some community and two-year colleges offer film study programs with courses in film and video editing. Universities with departments of broadcast journalism offer courses in film and video editing and also may have contacts at local television stations.

Much of the day-to-day work of film and television editors can be learned in an apprenticeship. By working closely with an editor, an apprentice can learn film operations and specific film-editing techniques.

Earnings

Film editors are not as highly paid as others working in their industry. They have less clout than directors or producers, but they have more authority in the production of a project than many other film industry workers. The median annual wage for film editors was \$68,680 in 2010, according to the U.S. Department of Labor. A small percentage of film editors earned less than \$26,000 a year, while some earned more than \$111,000. The most experienced and sought-after film editors can earn much higher salaries.

Outlook

It will be difficult to land a job as a film editor since many people want to enter the field. The growth of cable television, an increase in the number of independent film studios, and growing interest in American movies in other countries will create some new job opportunities for film editors.

And the Oscar Goes to...

The following editors have won the Oscar for best film editing in recent years:

2010: Angus Wall and Kirk Baxter, *The Social Network*
2009: Bob Murawski and Chris Innis, *The Hurt Locker*
2008: Chris Dickens, *Slumdog Millionaire*
2007: Christopher Rouse, *The Bourne Ultimatum*
2006: Thelma Schoonmaker, *The Departed*
2005: Hughes Winborne, *Crash*
2004: Thelma Schoonmaker, *The Aviator*
2003: Jamie Selkirk, *The Lord of the Rings: The Return of the King*
2002: Martin Walsh, *Chicago*
2001: Pietro Scalia, *Black Hawk Down*
2000: Stephen Mirrionen, *Traffic*

For more information on Academy Award-winning film editors, visit http://www.oscars.org/awardsdatabase.

FOR MORE INFO

The ACE offers career and education information for film editors at its Web site and sample articles from *CinemEditor* magazine.

American Cinema Editors (ACE)
100 Universal City Plaza
Verna Fields Building 2282, Room 190
Universal City, CA 91608-1002
818-777-2900
amercinema@earthlink.net
http://ace-filmeditors.org

For a variety of movie-related resources, visit the AFI Web site.

American Film Institute (AFI)
2021 North Western Avenue
Los Angeles, CA 90027-1657
323-856-7600
information@afi.com
http://www.afi.com

For information about union membership, contact

Motion Picture Editors Guild
International Alliance of Theatrical Stage Employees (IATSE Local 700)
7715 Sunset Boulevard, Suite 200
Hollywood, CA 90046-3912
323-876-4770
https://www.editorsguild.com

For information on sound editing, contact

Motion Picture Sound Editors
10061 Riverside Drive
PMB Box 751
Toluca Lake, CA 91602-2550
818-506-7731
mail@mpse.org
http://www.mpse.org

The digital revolution will greatly affect the editing process. Editors will work much more closely with visual effects experts in putting together projects. Digital technology may allow some prospective editors more direct routes into the industry, but the majority of editors will have to follow traditional routes, obtaining years of experience.

Film Extras

What Film Extras Do

Have you ever watched a movie with a big crowd scene that featured hundreds or even thousands of people? Or scenes of an airplane full of passengers or people walking down the street? These people are known as *film extras* or *background performers*. Extras, who usually do not have speaking roles, play an important role in establishing the world of the film. If there were no extras in scenes around the main actors, the story would not be believable.

Many people who want to work as *principal actors* (performers in featured roles) first work as extras to try to break into the industry. Others see work as an extra as a way to make a little extra money and get close to the film industry.

Film extras can advertise their availability for work by registering at a casting agency. On a day they can work, they simply contact the agency to see if it needs someone of their description (tall, short, dark hair, blonde hair, old, young, etc.).

Aspiring film extras can also attend open casting calls in their city when filming is taking place.

If selected, film extras receive instructions on what to bring to the set, and when and where to report to work. For most films, extras are asked to wear their own clothes. For a film set in another time period, they may have to report to the wardrobe department for a costume fitting. In some cases, a casting director for a film will be looking for specific types and talents. For example, if a scene features a basketball game, the director may need extras who can shoot free throws, dribble, and run up and down the court. Or a period scene in a dance hall may call for extras that know certain traditional dances. These extras are called *special ability extras* and usually receive better daily pay than general extras. A *stand-in* may also be needed for a film shoot. A stand-in is an extra who takes the place of a principal actor when the crew prepares to film a scene, but who is not actually filmed. Stand-ins are positioned on the set for the cameras to focus the shot and set up lights.

On the day of work, extras may be asked to participate in a rehearsal or they may simply jump right into the filming of a scene. They must follow the directions of the director and other staff. Extras may be asked to simply stand in the background, to talk with other extras, or to move freely about the set. Extras may have to repeat their actions, gestures, and expressions again and again until the filmmakers have the shot they need. Their scene may only take a few hours to complete or may take several days. Extras may be used for the background in only one scene or may be used in many scenes. In rare cases, an extra is picked from a crowd scene and given a line to speak. In this case, the performer is considered a *day player.*

Members of the Screen Actors Guild (SAG), the union for film actors and extras, generally receive better pay than nonunion extras. A film must have 30 SAG-registered extras on a given day before hiring nonunion extras.

Film extras play the role of football fans during the filming of a movie. (Greg Nelson, AP Photo)

Education and Training

Although you do not need a high school diploma to work as an extra, it is important that you earn one to help you prepare for college or land a job after graduation. High school classes that may be helpful to you in your work as an extra include theater, dance, physical education, and speech. You can work as an extra during your elementary school, middle school, and high school years.

Tips for Success

To be a successful film extra, you should

- be able to follow instructions
- be responsible and on time
- be attentive
- have patience
- be willing to work long hours.

If you want to eventually become an actor, it is a good idea to earn at least a bachelor's degree in theater or the dramatic arts.

Earnings

It is very rare that someone is able to make a living solely from work as an extra. According to SAG, a majority of its nearly 120,000 members make less than $7,500 a year. SAG sets daily wage minimums for its members, which vary according to city and type of extra work. For example, in 2010, extras made at least $139 a day. If they had a part showing off a special ability or talent, they were paid $149 or more a day. Extras also earn more if they have to work in rain or smoke, or if they are required to wear body makeup, wigs, or a certain haircut for the part. If they supply their own props, such as pets, cars, golf clubs, or

DID YOU KNOW?

- Approximately 2.4 million people in the United States worked in some area of the motion picture and television industries in 2008.
- More than 95,000 companies in all 50 states contributed to the film and television industries in some way in 2008.
- California and New York are the leading centers of film production in the United States. The top 10 production states outside of California and New York are Illinois, Texas, Florida, Georgia, Pennsylvania, New Jersey, North Carolina, Louisiana, Tennessee, and Massachusetts.

Source: Motion Picture Association of America

luggage, extras also are paid higher daily rates.

Any extra who is upgraded to a speaking part—even just one line of dialogue—is considered a day player and earns significantly more per day.

Outlook

It is hard to land a job in the film industry because many people want to work as extras and actors. Extras who live in New York or Los Angeles and have an extras agent will have better chances of landing a job. Breaking into the movie industry requires patience and determination. Aspiring extras who have these qualities will be the most successful.

FOR MORE INFO

For information about becoming an actor or extra, contact
Screen Actors Guild
5757 Wilshire Boulevard, 7th Floor
Los Angeles, CA 90036-3600
323-954-1600
saginfo@sag.org
http://www.sag.com

What Film Producers Do

The primary responsibility of *film producers* is to organize and obtain money to pay to make films. The job of a producer begins with the selection of a movie idea from a script (the written version of what happens in a film) or other material. Some films are made from original screenplays (the written story and dialogue of a movie), and others are adapted from books. If a book is selected, the producer first purchases the legal rights from

EXPLORING

- Read books about a career as a producer and the movie industry. See the Browse and Learn More section for suggestions.
- Join a film or video club.
- Organize your own movie. Hire your friends to work as "director," "camera operator," "screenwriter," and "actors" and oversee the production.

- Get involved in your school's theater productions, especially in a fund-raising capacity.
- Volunteer to work on committees that organize, produce, and publicize special events at your school or religious center.
- Talk to a producer about his or her career.

Producer Jerry Bruckheimer (center) discusses a scene with director Gore Verbinski (left) and actor Johnny Depp on the set of the film Pirates of the Caribbean: Dead Man's Chest. *(Disney Enterprises/Topham/The Image Works)*

the author or publishing company and hires a writer to adapt the book into a screenplay.

After selecting a project, the producer finds a director, technical crew, and lead actors to participate in the film. Along with the script and screenwriter, these essential people are referred to as *the package.* It is the package that the producer tries to sell to an investor to raise the necessary funds to finance the film.

There are three common sources for financing a film: major studios, production companies, and individual investors (wealthy people who are interested in funding a film). Major studios are the largest source of money and finance most of the big-budget films. Producers of documentary films approach individual donors; foundations; art agencies of federal, state, and local governments; and even family members and religious organizations.

Raising money from individual investors can occupy much of the producer's time. Fund-raising is done on the telephone as well as in conferences, at business lunches, and even at cocktail parties.

After raising the money, the producer takes the basic plan of the package and tries to work it into a developed project. The script may be rewritten several times, a full cast of actors is hired, salaries are negotiated, and the filming location is chosen.

During the production phase, the producer tries to keep the project on schedule and costs within the established budget. Other production tasks include the review of dailies, which are prints of the day's filming. As the head of the project, the

DID YOU KNOW?

- Motion picture cameras were invented in the late 1800s. The two earliest known films, made in 1888 by French-born Louis Le Prince, showed his father-in-law's garden and traffic crossing an English bridge.
- More advanced cameras and motion picture techniques quickly followed. In 1903 American director Edwin Porter and inventor Thomas Edison made *The Great Train Robbery*, one of the first movies in which scenes were filmed out of sequence. When the filming was completed, the scenes were edited and spliced together.
- By 1906, feature-length films were being made and many talented and financially savvy individuals were making their livings as producers. The first woman to become a producer was Alice Guy, who started the Solax Company in New York in 1910.

producer is responsible for resolving all problems, including personal conflicts such as those between the director and an actor, or the director and the studio. If the film is successfully completed, the producer monitors its distribution to theaters or release on DVD and may participate in the publicity and advertising of the film.

Many producers are self-employed. Others work as salaried employees of film companies, television stations, and television networks.

Education and Training

High school English composition and speech courses will help you develop writing and communication skills. Business and economics courses can prepare you for the financial responsibilities of a producer's job.

Many film producers have taken formal film courses at a college or a university or have graduated with film-related degrees. There are more than 1,000 colleges, universities, and trade schools that offer classes or degrees in film studies. However, experience is the best qualification. Most producers work their way into the position from other film-related jobs, such as production, acting, editing, and directing. It is important to have contacts in the industry and with potential investors.

Earnings

Film producers are generally paid a portion of the project's profits or a fee negotiated between the producer and a studio. The U.S. Department of Labor reports that movie producers earned an average salary of $109,860 in 2010. Those just starting out in the field earned less than $33,000. Producers of highly successful films can earn $1 million or more, while those who make low-budget documentary films might earn considerably less than the average. Entry-level production assistants can earn from less than minimum wage to $20,000 per year.

DID YOU KNOW?

- Approximately 4,000 motion picture, television, and new media producers are members of the Producers Guild of America.
- A large number of producers work in Los Angeles and New York City.
- About 21 percent of producers are self-employed.

Sources: Producers Guild of America, U.S. Department of Labor

Outlook

Opportunities for producers may increase with the expansion of cable and satellite television, increasing video and DVD rentals, and growing overseas demand for American-made films, but competition for jobs will be strong. Since many people want to work in the movie industry, it will be hard to land a good job. Producers with a lot of experience and many industry contacts will have the best job prospects.

FOR MORE INFO

For industry information, contact
Alliance of Motion Picture and Television Producers
15301 Ventura Boulevard, Building E
Sherman Oaks, CA 91403-5885
818-995-3600
http://www.amptp.org

For film news and information on educational programs, visit the AFI Web site or contact
American Film Institute (AFI)
2021 North Western Avenue
Los Angeles, CA 90027-1657

323-856-7600
information@afi.com
http://www.afi.com

Visit the FAQ section of the PGA Web site to read about producer careers.
Producers Guild of America (PGA)
8530 Wilshire Boulevard, Suite 450
Beverly Hills, CA 90211-3115
310-358-9020
info@producersguild.org
http://www.producersguild.org

Lighting Technicians

What Lighting Technicians Do

Lighting technicians set up and control the lighting equipment for movie and television productions. These technicians are sometimes known as *assistant chief set electricians* or *lights operators*. The head lighting technician is known as a *gaffer. Best boys* (both male and female) assist gaffers with their duties.

When a movie shoot is being planned, lighting technicians talk with the director to find out what types of lighting and special lighting effects will be used. Lighting technicians then arrange the equipment they will need to produce the required lighting effects. For example, if the script calls for sunshine to be streaming through a window, technicians set up lights to produce this effect. Other effects they may be asked to produce include lighting the flash from an explosion or the soft glow of a room lit with old-fashioned oil lamps.

EXPLORING

- Work the lighting for a school stage production.
- Join your school's newspaper or yearbook staff and practice working with cameras. Experiment with different lighting options.
- Ask if you can record a school play, concert, or sporting event. Before the event, figure out what lighting will be used and how to best film it.
- Talk to a lighting technician about his or her career.

Lighting technicians prepare lights and rigging for a scene. (Jim Damaske, The Image Works/*St. Petersburg Times*)

The amount of work done by lighting technicians depends on the movie's budget. If the production is small, the technicians will set up the lights themselves. For blockbuster movie shoots, best boys and other assistants set up the lights following the lighting technician's instructions.

During the filming, lighting technicians work in a control room and follow a special script. The script tells them which lighting effects are needed at what times during the shoot.

During filming, the lighting technicians watch the shoot on television monitors in the control room. This allows them to see their work and to make any necessary adjustments.

Setting up lights can be heavy work, especially when lighting a large movie set. Technicians should be able to handle heavy lights on stands and work with suspended lights while on a ladder. They should be able to work with electricians' hand tools (screwdrivers, pliers, and so forth) and know how to safely work with electricity. Lighting technicians should also be dependable and capable of working as part of a team.

DID YOU KNOW?

- In 2008, nearly 54 percent of workers in the industry were age 34 and younger. This is a much higher percentage than the average for all industries.
- Employment in the industry is expected to grow by 14 percent from 2008 to 2018—slightly faster than the average growth rate for all industries.

Source: Motion Picture Association of America, U.S. Department of Labor

Education and Training

In high school, you should learn as much as possible about electronics, film history, and working with lighting (by participating in theater productions). Courses in physics and math are also important. English and speech classes will help you develop good communication skills. These are essential for working with the various people on the movie set.

After high school, attend a community college or technical school that offers a program in electronics and broadcast technology. If you would like to rise to a technical management position, you should consider earning a college degree in electrical or electronics engineering.

Earnings

Salaries for lighting technicians vary according to the technician's experience. Annual income is also determined by the number of projects a technician handles a year. The most ex-

Lights

Need a baby-baby? A midget? A nooklite? An inbetweenie? Visit http://www.mole.com, the Web site for the Mole-Richardson Co., to read about lighting equipment used in Hollywood. At the site, you'll see pictures of a variety of different kinds of lighting products in its online catalog, and get a sense of some of the lingo of the profession.

perienced technicians can work year-round on a variety of projects, while those starting out may go weeks without work. Audio and video equipment technicians (a category that includes those who work with lighting) earned salaries that ranged from less than $23,000 to $73,000 or more in 2010, according to the U.S. Department of Labor. Those employed in the motion picture and video industries had mean annual earnings of $47,950.

Outlook

As long as the movie and television industries continue to grow, opportunities will remain available for people who wish to become lighting technicians. With the expansion of the cable television market, lighting technicians may find work in more than one industry. However, persistence and hard work are required in order to secure a good job in film. The increasing use of visual effects and computer-generated imagery will likely have an impact on the work of lighting technicians. Through computer programs, filmmakers and editors can create lighting effects themselves. However, live-action shots are still necessary in the filmmaking process, and will remain so for some time. Getting the initial shots of a film requires sophisticated lighting equipment and trained technicians. Lighting technicians often have to know about the assembly and operation of more pieces of equipment than anyone else working on a production. In the future, equipment will become more compact and mobile, making the technician's job easier.

FOR MORE INFO

To read interviews with filmmakers, visit the AFI Web site.

American Film Institute (AFI)
2021 North Western Avenue
Los Angeles, CA 90027-1657
323-856-7600
information@afi.com
http://www.afi.com

Visit this site for interviews with award-winning cinematographers, a "tricks of the trade" page, information about film schools, multimedia presentations, and the *American Cinematographer* online magazine.

American Society of Cinematographers
PO Box 2230
Hollywood, CA 90078-2230
800-448-0145
office@theasc.com
http://www.theasc.com

For education and training information, contact

Studio Electrical Lighting Technicians
International Alliance of Theatrical Stage Employees (IATSE Local 728)
1001 West Magnolia Boulevard
Burbank, CA 91506-1606
818-954-0728
http://www.iatse728.org

What Makeup Artists Do

Makeup artists apply makeup to actors and models. They work in the movie, television, fashion, and commercial industries. They also work in theatrical productions.

Makeup artists design and apply makeup for screen and stage actors. They read scripts and meet with directors, producers, and special effects technicians. They create makeup and special effects such as scars and prosthetics (artificial body parts). Sometimes makeup artists apply "clean" (natural-look-

EXPLORING

- Read *The Artisan* magazine (http://www.local706.org/artisan.cfm) to learn about makeup artists who work in the film and television industries.
- Look for opportunities to volunteer your help to local theaters. The summer months will offer the most opportunities. Small community the-aters will pay little or nothing, but they may allow you the best chance to explore makeup artistry.
- Volunteer to do makeup for school theater productions. Make sure to take pictures of your work.
- Talk with a makeup artist about his or her work.

ing) makeup and eliminate or apply wrinkles, tattoos, or scars. When they design makeup, makeup artists must consider the age of the characters, the setting and period of the film or play, and the lighting effects that will be used. Historical productions require considerable research to design hair, makeup, and fashion styles of a particular era. Makeup artists also may work on hair, but in many states locally licensed cosmetologists must be brought in for hair cutting, coloring, and perms.

Makeup artists play an important role during filming as well. For example, they observe actors during filming to make sure their makeup is just right. They reapply or adjust makeup as needed during filming. They help the actors remove makeup at the end of the day.

Most makeup artists are self-employed and work on a freelance basis. Freelance makeup artists must handle all the administrative tasks that go with running a business. These include arranging job appointments, running errands, invoicing clients, updating their portfolio and Web sites, and shopping for supplies in stores and online.

Education and Training

To prepare for a career as a makeup artist, take art classes, such as art history, photography, painting, drawing, and sculpting. Anatomy and chemistry classes will also be useful. Participate in school drama productions. Assist with makeup whenever possible.

Cosmetology licenses or certificates from special makeup schools are not required, but they may help, especially when you start out. If you are willing to spend some time working for very little pay, or even for free, you can gain valuable experience assisting an experienced, established makeup artist. There are also some highly regarded schools for makeup artists, such as the Joe Blasco Makeup Schools in California and Florida.

A makeup artist prepares an actor for a scene in a movie. (Matthias Rietschel, AP Photo)

Earnings

Makeup artists usually earn a daily rate of pay for their services. This rate varies depending on the budget and size of the production and the experience and reputation of the makeup artist. Day rates can range from $50 for a small theater production or independent movie to $1,000 for a feature film. Work is rarely steady. Most makeup artists work long hours for several weeks, and then may be without work for a time.

Movie makeup artists who worked full time had mean annual salaries of $80,250 in 2010, according to the U.S. Department of Labor. Salaries for all makeup artists ranged from less than $18,000 to more than $102,000. However, celebrity artists can earn salaries of more than $125,000 annually.

Outlook

It will be hard to land a job as a movie makeup artist because the field is relatively small and many people want to enter it. Despite the strong competition, new jobs will become available as the film and television industries continue to grow. Increased use of special effects will require makeup artists with specialized talent and training. On the other hand, the growing popularity of computer-generated effects in movies and television shows will reduce the number of makeup artists needed for some productions.

Tips for Success

To be a successful makeup artist, you should

- have patience
- be able to work well with others
- have artistic ability
- be attentive to detail
- be able to work well under deadline pressure
- have business skills
- be able to accept constructive criticism regarding your work
- be confident of your abilities

DID YOU KNOW?

- The largest movie studios by market share in 2009 were 1) Warner Bros.; 2) Paramount; 3) Sony/Columbia; 4) 20th Century Fox; 5) Buena Vista; and 6) Universal.
- In 2009, the average admission price for a family of four to the movies was $28.72.
- There are about 40,000 movie screens in 7,000 theaters in the United States.

Source: Visual Effects Society

FOR MORE INFO

For information on union membership, contact
International Alliance of Theatrical Stage Employees, Moving Picture Technicians, Artists and Allied Crafts of the United States, Its Territories, and Canada
1430 Broadway, 20th Floor
New York, NY 10018-3348
212-730-1770
http://www.iatse-intl.org

This local union of the International Alliance of Theatrical Stage Employees, Moving Picture Technicians, Artists and Allied Crafts of the United States, Its Territories, and Canada represents the professional interests of makeup artists and hair stylists who work in film and television. Visit its Web site for more information.

Make-Up Artists & Hair Stylists Guild Local 706
http://www.local706.org

For information on theatrical careers, contact
Theatre Communications Group
520 Eighth Avenue, 24th Floor
New York, NY 10018-4156
212-609-5900
tcg@tcg.org
http://www.tcg.org

For information about the Joe Blasco Makeup Schools and careers in makeup artistry, visit
Joe Blasco Makeup Schools
http://www.joeblasco.com

Makeup artists with advanced training, strong artistic skills, and the ability to find work in multiple industries will have the best job prospects.

Media Planners and Buyers

What Media Planners and Buyers Do

Once a movie is completed, an advertising campaign must be created to encourage people to watch it. *Media specialists* place advertisements that will reach specific groups of customers and get the best response from the market for the least amount of money. Within the media department, *media planners* gather information about the sizes and types of audiences that can be reached through each of the various media (print, television, Internet, billboards, etc.) and about the cost of advertising in each medium. *Media buyers* purchase space in printed publications, on billboards and the Internet, and on radio or television stations. Advertising media workers are supervised by a *media director,* who is accountable for the overall media plan. In addition to advertising agencies, media planners and buyers work for large companies, such as film studios, that purchase space or broadcast time. These media specialists must be familiar with the markets that each medium reaches, as well as the advantages and disadvantages of advertising in each.

Media planners determine target markets based on their clients' advertising needs. For example, if a movie studio wanted to advertise its new *Harry Potter* movie, media planners would gather information about the public's viewing, reading, and buying habits by administering questionnaires and conducting other forms of market research. Through this research, planners would identify target markets (in this case, children, readers of the *Harry Potter* books, etc.) by sorting data according to people's ages, interests, leisure activities, and other categories.

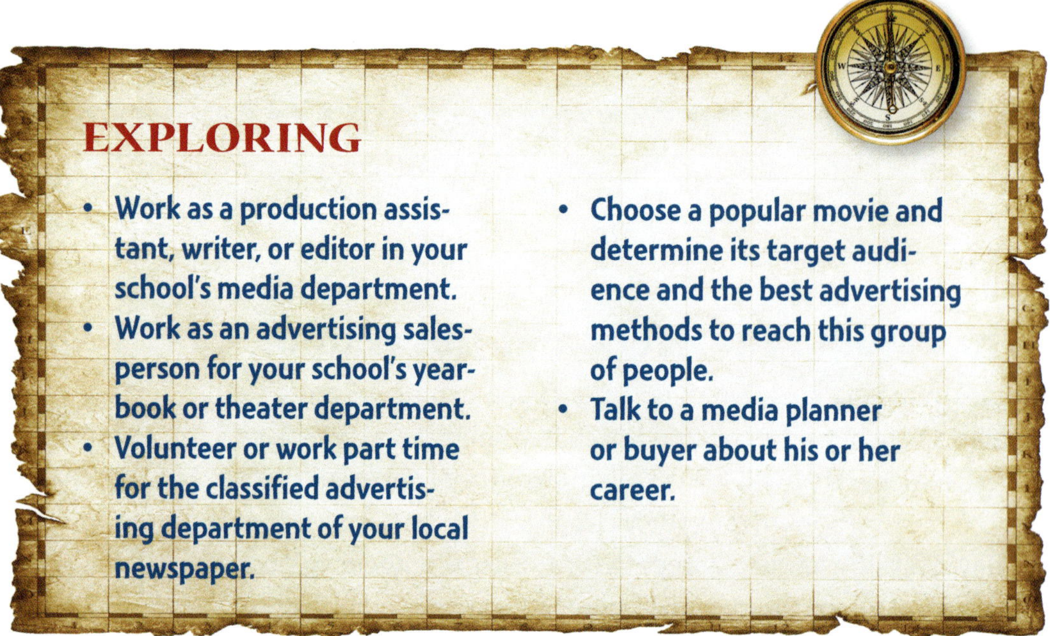

By knowing which groups of people watch certain shows, listen to specific radio stations, or read particular magazines or newspapers, media planners can help the movie studio select airtime or print space to reach the consumers most likely to watch the movie. For example, Saturday morning television shows attract children, while prime-time programs often draw family audiences. These would be excellent places to advertise the new *Harry Potter* movie since these groups make up a large segment of potential viewers.

Media buyers do the actual purchasing of the time on radio or television or the space in a newspaper or magazine in which an advertisement will run. In addition to tracking the time and space available for purchase, media buyers ensure that ads appear when and where they should, negotiate costs for ad placement, and calculate rates, usage, and budgets. They also maintain contact with clients, keeping them informed of all advertising-related developments and resolving any conflicts that arise.

Workers who actually sell the print space or airtime to advertisers are called *print sales workers* or *broadcast time salespeople.* Like media planners, these professionals know a lot about the target markets served by their organizations and can often provide useful information about editorial content or broadcast programs.

In contrast to print and broadcast planners and buyers, *interactive media specialists* manage all critical aspects of their clients' online advertising campaigns. While interactive media planners may have responsibilities similar to those of print or broadcast planners, they also act as *new technology specialists,* placing and tracking all online ads and maintaining relationships with clients and webmasters alike.

Tips for Success

To be a successful media planner or buyer, you should

- have a strong understanding of the movie business and the buying habits of the public
- have good problem-solving abilities
- be creative
- have excellent communication skills
- be able to work well with others as a member of a team
- have the ability to handle multiple assignments

Education and Training

You can prepare for a future job as media planner and/or buyer by taking specific courses in high school such as business, marketing, advertising, radio and television, and film and video. General liberal arts classes, such as economics, English, communications, and journalism, are also important, since media planners and buyers must be able to communicate clearly with both clients and coworkers. In addition, math classes will give you the skills to work with budget figures and placement costs.

Words to Learn

advertisement a paid announcement of a product or service to the public

advertising agency a group of researchers, writers, artists, buyers of space and time, other specialists, and account executives who design and execute advertising programs for clients

electronic banners the Internet's equivalent of billboard advertising, which accounts for 80 percent of online ads

market research the study of consumer groups to determine personal interests and characteristics

media the avenues through which advertisers can place ads, including the Internet, television, radio, magazines, newspapers, and outdoor signs

target audience a group of consumers that is considered the most likely to purchase a product; also known as target market

time slot the specific time that a commercial will air on television or radio

Most media positions require a bachelor's degree, often with majors in marketing or advertising. Even if you have prior work experience or training in media, you should select college classes that provide a good balance of business course work; broadcast, print, and Internet experience; and liberal arts studies.

Earnings

Because media planners and buyers work for a variety of companies all across the country and the world, earnings can vary greatly. Advertising sales agents employed in the movie industry had mean annual earnings of $63,980 in 2010, according to the U.S. Department of Labor. Salaries for all advertising sales agents ranged from less than $23,000 to more than $96,000. Media directors can earn between $46,000 and $120,000,

FOR MORE INFO

For profiles of advertising workers and career information, contact
Advertising Educational Foundation
220 East 42nd Street, Suite 3300
New York, NY 10017-5806
212-986-8060
http://www.aef.com

For information on the advertising industry, contact
American Advertising Federation
1101 Vermont Avenue, NW, Suite 500
Washington, DC 20005-6306

800-999-2231
aaf@aaf.org
http://www.aaf.org

For information on advertising agencies, contact
American Association of Advertising Agencies
405 Lexington Avenue, 18th Floor
New York, NY 10174-1801
212-682-2500
http://www.aaaa.org

depending on the type of employer and the director's experience level.

Outlook

The employment outlook for media planners and buyers, like the outlook for the advertising industry itself, depends on the general health of the economy. When the economy is strong, companies produce an increasing number of goods and seek to promote them via newspapers, magazines, television, radio, the Internet, and various other media. The U.S. Department of Labor anticipates that employment in the advertising industry will be fair in coming years.

Competition for all advertising positions, including entry-level jobs, is expected to be intense. Media planners and buyers who have a lot of experience will have the best chances of finding a job.

Movie Writers and Critics

What Movie Writers and Critics Do

"That movie was great!" "No, it stunk!" "It was OK, but I really liked…" Everyone seems to have an opinion about movies today. But did you know that some people make a career out of writing and talking about movies? *Movie writers* express their ideas about movies in words for books, magazines, newspapers, advertisements, radio, television, and the Internet. These writing jobs require a combination of creativity and hard work. Movie writers are also known as *movie reporters* and *authors.* (For information about writers who create scripts for films, see the article on Screenwriters.) Good movie writers gather as much information as possible about the subject and then carefully check the accuracy of their sources. This can involve extensive library research; interviews with actors, directors, and other movie industry workers; visits to movie sets; and watching a lot of movies. Writers usually keep notes from which they prepare an outline or summary. They use this outline to write a first draft and then rewrite sections of their material, always searching for the best way to express their ideas. Generally, their writing will be reviewed, corrected, and revised many times by an editor before a final copy is ready for publication.

Movie critics review films for print publications, Web sites, and television and radio stations. They review all types of new movies—from comedies and dramas, to documentaries and foreign films, to animated shorts. Critics watch the movies they plan to review at special screenings or via advance DVD copies

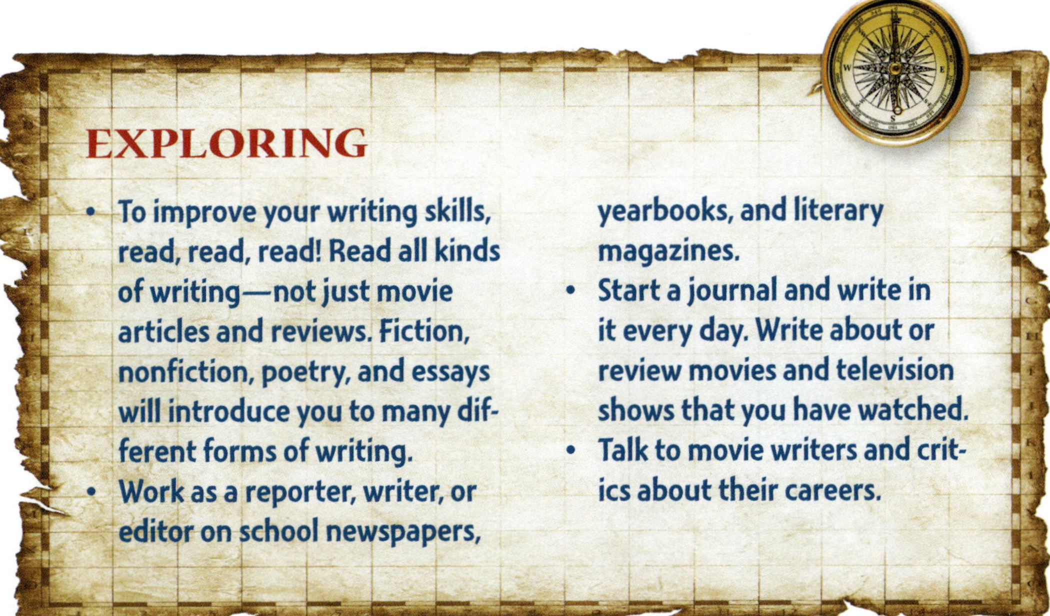

that they can view at home or in the office. When reviewing a movie, a critic takes into account many factors. They analyze the story line; performance of the actors; quality of the movie's direction, editing, and special effects; and overall entertainment value. They determine if the movie met standards they have established in these categories and often assign a rating to the movie. Their reviews are read or listened to by many people who want advice on what movie to see.

Education and Training

In high school, take English, journalism, and communications courses. To gain a better understanding of movies, take classes in broadcasting and film, if they are available. Other useful courses include computer science and typing.

A college education is usually necessary if you want to become a writer or critic. You should also know how to use a computer for word processing and be able to handle the pres-

Tips for Success

To be a successful movie writer or critic, you should

- **have a strong love of and interest in the movies**
- **have excellent writing skills**
- **be opinionated**
- **be a good researcher**
- **be an expert at grammar and punctuation**
- **have strong communication skills**
- **be able to meet deadlines**
- **enjoy meeting and interacting with others**
- **be willing to accept criticism from the public, who may not agree with your opinions**

sure of deadlines. Employers prefer to hire people who have a communications, English, or journalism degree. Movie writers and critics must know a lot about their subject, so film classes are also useful. Some writers and editors may have a college degree in film, drama, film directing, film production, or a related field in addition to a degree in English, journalism, or communications.

Earnings

Most writers earned between $29,000 and $109,000 a year in 2010, according to the U.S. Department of Labor (DOL). Writers working in the motion picture industry had mean annual earnings of $78,680.

The DOL loosely categorizes critics under the heading of reporter. According to the DOL, the median annual salary for reporters was $34,530 in 2010. Salaries ranged from less than $20,000 to $75,000 or more. In the same year, reporters who worked in radio and television broadcasting had average annual earnings of $53,590. Those employed by newspaper, periodical, book, and directory publishers earned $33,420.

DID YOU KNOW?

Opening Soon at a Theater Near You was the first film review television show in the United States. It debuted on September 4, 1975, and was hosted by movie critics Roger Ebert and Gene Siskel. *Opening Soon* started as a local show on WTTW, a public broadcasting station in Chicago. In 1977, the show went national, and its name was changed to *Sneak Previews*. The show was very popular during its time, and aired on more than 180 stations. *Sneak Previews* made stars out of Ebert and Siskel. They became some of the most well-known movie critics in the world. Siskel passed away in 1999. Ebert continues to review movies for the *Chicago Sun-Times*, and writes books about the movie industry. Visit http://rogerebert.suntimes.com to read Ebert's movie reviews.

Outlook

Employment for writers is expected to be good during the next decade. Jobs should be available at newspapers, magazines, book publishers, advertising agencies, businesses, Web sites, and nonprofit organizations. The best job opportunities will be found at small newspapers, radio stations, and television stations. In these organizations, pay is low even by the standards of the publishing business.

Many people want to become movie writers and critics. This makes it difficult to land a job in the field—especially because there are only a small number of positions available. Writers and critics with previous experience and specialized education in film studies and reporting will have the best chances of finding jobs.

FOR MORE INFO

Visit the association's Web site to learn more about the book business.

Association of American Publishers
71 Fifth Avenue, 2nd Floor
New York, NY 10003-3004
212-255-0200
http://www.publishers.org

This organization is a good source of information about the magazine industry.

Association of Magazine Media
810 Seventh Avenue, 24th Floor
New York, NY 10019-5873
212-872-3700
mpa@magazine.org
http://www.magazine.org

The association represents nearly 200 television, radio, and online critics in the United States and Canada.

Broadcast Film Critics Association
9220 Sunset Boulevard, Suite 220
Los Angeles, CA 90069-3503
310-860-2665
info@bfca.org
http://www.bfca.org/about.php

For information on the Golden Globe Awards, contact

Hollywood Foreign Press Association
646 North Robertson Boulevard
West Hollywood, CA 90069-5022
info@hfpa.org
http://www.goldenglobes.org

For information on careers in the newspaper industry, contact

Newspaper Association of America
4401 Wilson Boulevard, Suite 900
Arlington, VA 22203-1867
571-366-1000
http://www.naa.org

The OFCS is an international association of Internet-based film critics and journalists.

Online Film Critics Society (OFCS)
gc@ofcs.org
http://www.ofcs.org

Visit the following Web site for detailed information about journalism careers:

High School Journalism
http://www.hsj.org

Production Assistants

What Production Assistants Do

Production assistants perform a variety of tasks for movie, television, and video producers and other staff members. As a production assistant you will not be famous like actors or directors, but work in this career will give you the experience and contacts to advance in the movie industry.

Production assistants' duties range from making sure a Hollywood star has coffee in the morning to stopping street traffic so a director can film a scene. They photocopy scripts for actors, help set up equipment, and perform other menial tasks. The best production assistants know where to be at the right time to make themselves useful.

Some production assistants keep production files in order. These files include contracts, budgets, page changes (old pages from a script that has been revised), and other records. The documents must be kept organized and accessible for whenever the producer may need them.

Production assistants may also have to keep the producer's production folder in order and up-to-date. The production folder contains everything the producer needs to know about the production at a glance. Production assistants make sure the folder includes the shooting schedule, the most recent version of the budget, cast and crew lists with phone numbers or email addresses, a phone sheet detailing all production-related phone calls the producer needs to make, and the up-to-date shooting script. As new versions of these forms are created, production

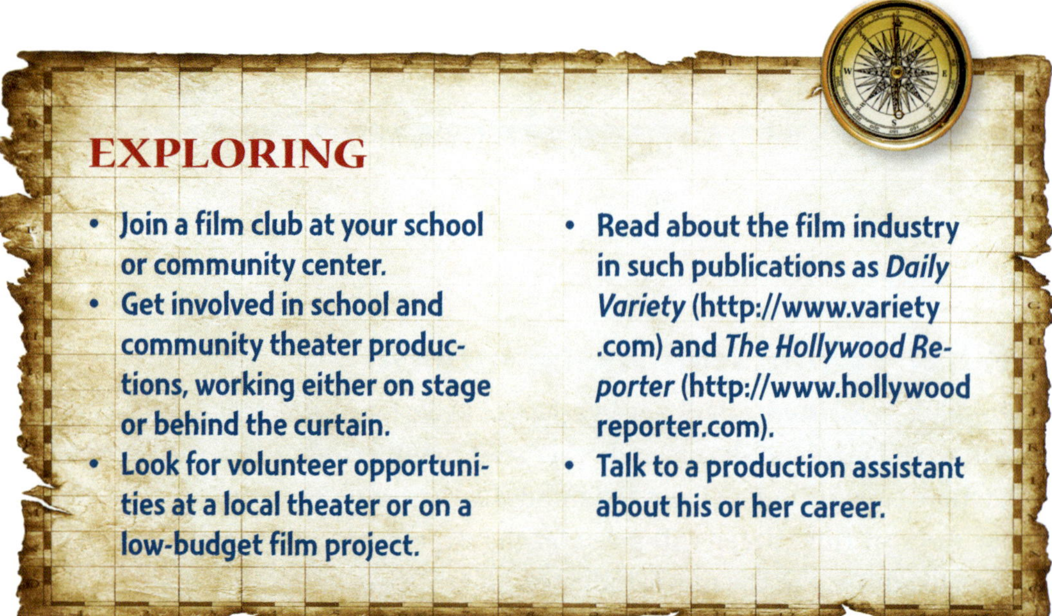

EXPLORING

- Join a film club at your school or community center.
- Get involved in school and community theater productions, working either on stage or behind the curtain.
- Look for volunteer opportunities at a local theater or on a low-budget film project.
- Read about the film industry in such publications as *Daily Variety* (http://www.variety.com) and *The Hollywood Reporter* (http://www.hollywoodreporter.com).
- Talk to a production assistant about his or her career.

assistants update the producer's folder and file the older versions for reference. This information may also be maintained in a computer database.

Production assistants schedule an hour or so in a producer's schedule to watch the dailies (the film shot each day) and make related calls to discuss them with other staff members. Production assistants make travel and hotel reservations and arrange for rehearsal space. They run errands and pass along messages for producers, directors, actors, musicians, and other members of the technical crew.

Production assistants often get stuck with undesirable tasks such as sweeping floors, guarding movie sets, or errands such as finding a particular brand of green tea for a demanding actress. However, a successful film shoot could not happen without production assistants on the set.

Education and Training

In high school, take courses in photography, film, broadcast journalism, and media to learn about the film industry. Business, typing, speech, and computer science classes will also be useful.

There are no formal education requirements for production assistants. Most production assistants consider the position a stepping-stone into other careers in the industry. You learn much of what you'll need to know on the set of a film, following the instructions of crew members and other assistants. Many film students work part time or on a contract basis as production assistants to gain experience while they are still in school. There are many good undergraduate programs in film and video with concentrations in such areas as directing, acting, editing, producing, screenwriting, cinematography, broadcast engineering, and television.

Tips for Success

To be a successful production assistant, you should

- be able to follow directions
- have good organizational skills
- be able to work well with others
- be enthusiastic
- be a quick learner
- be able to sit quietly during down-time or filming

Earnings

Because working as a production assistant is the starting point for most professionals and artists in the film industry, many people volunteer their time until they make connections and move into paid positions. Those assistants who can negotiate payment may make between $200 and $400 a week, but they

All in a Day's Work

If, after reading this list, you still want to pursue a production assistant job, you may just have what it takes to make it as a production assistant. Following are some possible tasks on any given day:

- Purchasing, washing, chopping, and arranging 20 pounds of fruits and veggies for the cast and crew snack table.
- Purchasing $200 worth of extra fancy ketchup and then submerging an actor's costume in it.
- Watching videos for hours to make sure that there aren't any technical glitches.
- Leaving the set every hour to insert more quarters in the meter where the director's car is parked.
- Driving around the city all day delivering scripts.
- Cleaning up dog/cat/horse/cheetah/lizard "messes" after an animal show.
- Sitting around, doing absolutely nothing until you are needed.

may only have the opportunity to work on a few projects a year. Production assistants working full time in an office may start at around $20,000 a year, but with experience can make around $65,000.

Outlook

There will always be a need for assistants in movie production. However, competition for jobs can be tough, since it is such a good entry-level position for someone who wants to make connections and learn about the movie industry. Fortunately, production assistants usually do not stay in their jobs more than one or two years, so turnover is fairly high. Production assistants will find employment anywhere a movie, television show, or video is being filmed, but more opportunities exist in Los Angeles and New York City. There may be opportunities at local television stations or smaller production companies that produce educational and corporate videos and movies.

FOR MORE INFO

For a variety of movie-related resources, visit the AFI Web site.
American Film Institute (AFI)
2021 North Western Avenue
Los Angeles, CA 90027-1657
323-856-7600
information@afi.com
http://www.afi.com

Production Designers and Art Directors

What Production Designers and Art Directors Do

Production designers oversee the overall look of the visual elements in movies, television broadcasts, and commercials. They approve the props, costumes, and locations. They are experts in filmmaking and video production techniques, design, computer graphics, and animation, depending on their specialty. Production designers also work on stage productions. In the movie and television industries, *art directors* are the top assistants of production designers. They make sure that the production designer's goals for the project are enacted.

Production designers and art directors for film, television, and other broadcast media have many responsibilities. If the movie or television show is to be shot on location, the production designer works with a location scout to find a location that best

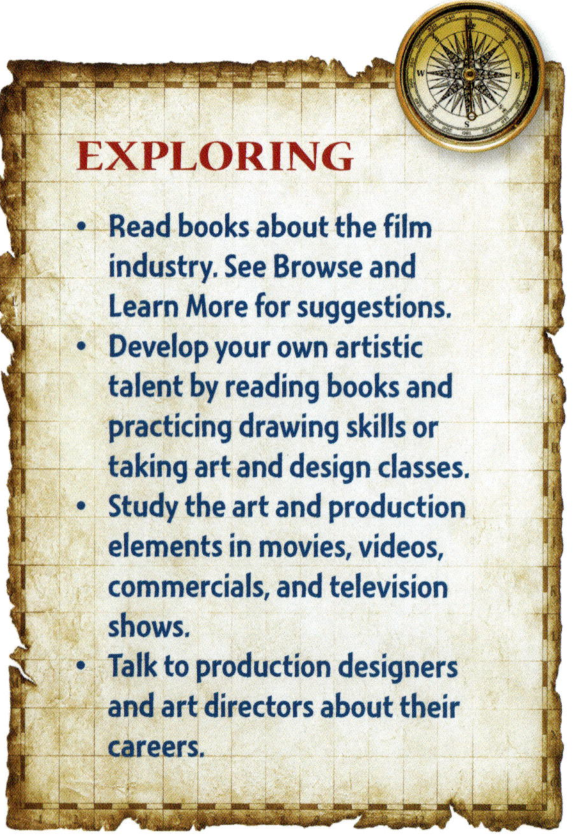

fits the setting depicted in the script and works with the budget of the project. Then they submit several rough drawings, called storyboards, which show step by step what the filmed piece will look like when it is finished. The storyboards are drawn by hand or with the help of software drawing programs. During this time, they also work with the production manager and line producer to lock down a budget for the art department so that construction on the sets can begin. Once the budget is approved, the sets are built.

During the various stages of production, the production designer manages the talents of many workers. These include art directors, set decorators and designers, model makers, location managers, propmasters, construction coordinators, and special effects people. They also work with writers, unit production managers, cinematographers, costume designers, and post-production staff, including editors.

To be a successful production designer or art director, you should be creative and imaginative, able to work with all sorts of specialized equipment and computer software, and have the ability to get along well with different types of people. You should also be able to handle stress and pressure, have good time management skills, and be willing to travel when filming on location.

Education and Training

To prepare for a career as a production designer or art director, concentrate on art and computer classes, as well as math. Production designers and art directors in film and broadcasting earn degrees in production design, film, directing, animation, or cinematography.

The positions of production designer and art director are not entry level. People in these professions typically gain expe-

DID YOU KNOW?

Where Production Designers and Art Directors Work

- advertising agencies
- computer game developers
- film and television production houses
- film and television studios
- marketing and public relations firms
- multimedia developers
- publishing companies
- theater companies
- other organizations that produce or use visual elements

rience by working as production assistants or art department assistants. As they gain experience and learn the ins and outs of the movie industry, they move into higher positions.

Earnings

The average salary for movie art directors was $125,010 in 2010, according to the U.S. Department of Labor. Entry-level art

Words to Learn

art department a collection of professionals (production designer, art director, set director, and others) who work with the visual aspects and designs of a movie

costumes clothing and accessories worn by actors

location a place away from the film studio where a movie is filmed

prop an item worn or used by actors in a scene such as tools, weapons, clothing, jewelry, etc.

storyboards rough drawings that show step by step what the filmed piece will look like when it is finished

FOR MORE INFO

For industry information, contact
Art Directors Club
106 West 29th Street
New York, NY 10001-5301
212-643-1440
info@adcglobal.org
http://www.adcglobal.org

For information on art directors who are employed in the movie industry, contact
Art Directors Guild & Scenic, Title, and Graphic Artists
11969 Ventura Boulevard, 2nd Floor
Studio City, CA 91604-2630

818-762-9995
http://www.adg.org

This union represents production designers, art directors, and other film industry professionals working in film, television, industrial shows, theater, opera, ballet, commercials, and exhibitions. Visit its Web site for more information.
United Scenic Artists Local 829
29 West 38th Street, 15th Floor
New York, NY 10018-5504
212-581-0300
http://www.usa829.org

directors in all industries earned less than $43,000 a year, while very experienced art directors earned more than $163,000 a year.

The weekly base pay for a motion picture art director who is a member of the International Alliance of Theatrical Stage Employees is approximately $3,000. Top production designers can earn salaries of more than $10,000 per week. Production designers who work on nonunion productions typically earn less money.

Outlook

Employment for production designers and art directors in the movie and television industries is expected to be only fair. Many people want to enter these industries, but only the most talented and hard-working people will be able to land jobs.

What Screenwriters Do

A screenplay details everything that happens in a movie, including dialogue, video and audio instructions, and the movements of the actors. *Screenwriters* write scripts for movies and television shows. The themes may be their own ideas or stories assigned by a producer or director. Often, screenwriters are hired to turn, or adapt, popular plays or novels into screenplays. Writers of original screenplays create their own stories, which are produced for the movie industry or television. Screenwriters may also write television programs, such as comedies, dramas, documentaries, variety shows, and entertainment specials.

Screenwriters must not only be creative, but they must also have great research skills. For projects such as historical movies, documentaries, and medical or science programs, research is a very important step.

Screenwriters start with an outline, or a treatment, of the story's plot. Scripts are written in a two-column format. One column is used for dialogue and sound, the other for video instructions. One page of script equals about one minute of running time, though it varies. Each page has about 150 words and takes about 20 seconds to read. When the director or producer approves the story outline, screenwriters then complete the story for production. During the writing process, screenwriters write many drafts (versions) of the script. They meet frequently with directors and producers to discuss script changes.

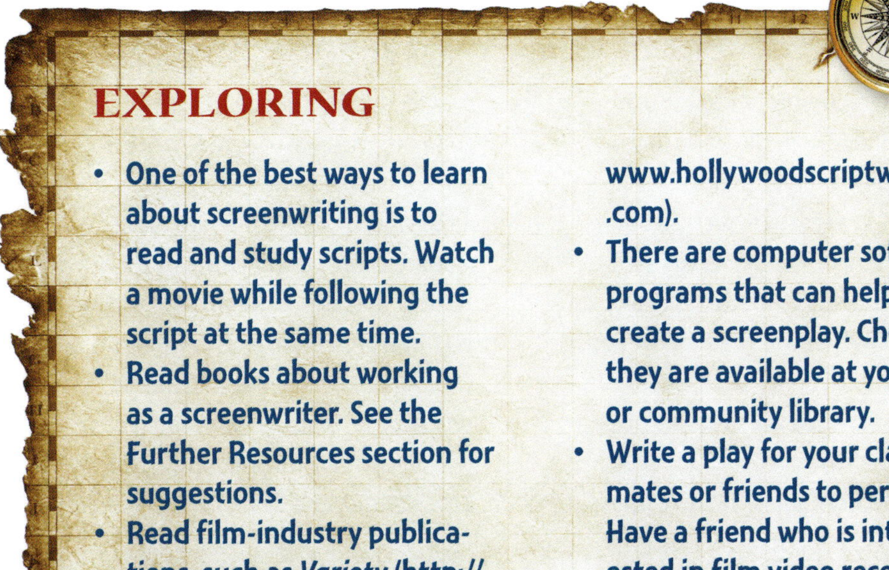

Some screenwriters work alone and others work with a team of writers. Many specialize in certain types of scripts, such as dramas, comedies, and documentaries. *Motion picture screenwriters* usually write alone and exclusively for movies.

Education and Training

In high school, you should develop your writing skills in English, theater, speech, and journalism classes. Social studies and foreign language classes can also be helpful in creating interesting scripts. Other important classes include history, psychology, and computer science.

DID YOU KNOW?

Women screenwriters were much more prominent in the early days of filmmaking. Half of the films made before 1925 were written by women, such as Frances Marion (*Stella Dallas, The Scarlet Letter*) and Anita Loos (*The Women*). Marion was the highest paid screenwriter from 1916 to the 1930s, and she served as the first vice president of the Writer's Guild. Though a smaller percentage of feature films written by women are produced today, more women screenwriters have won Academy Awards since 1985 than in all the previous years. Among recent Oscar winners are Ruth Prawer Jhabvala (*A Room with a View* and *Howard's End*), Jane Campion (*The Piano*), Callie Khouri (*Thelma and Louise*), Emma Thompson (*Sense and Sensibility*), Sofia Coppola *(Lost in Translation)*, and Diablo Cody *(Juno)*.

Important qualities for a screenwriter include a creative imagination and the ability to tell a story. The best way to prepare for a career as a screenwriter is to write and read every day. A college degree is not required, but a liberal arts education is helpful because it exposes you to a wide range of subjects. Some colleges offer degrees in screenwriting or film studies. While in school, become involved in theater to learn about all of the elements required by a screenplay, such as characters, plots, and themes. Book clubs, creative writing classes, and film study are also good ways to learn the basic elements of screenwriting.

Earnings

Annual wages for screenwriters vary widely. Some screenwriters make hundreds of thousands of dollars from their scripts. Others write and film their own scripts without receiving any payment at all, relying on backers and loans. Screenwriters who work independently do not earn regular salaries. They are paid a fee for each script they write. Those who write for ongoing television shows do earn regular salaries. According to the Writers Guild of America (WGA) 2008 Theatrical and Television Basic Agreement, earnings for writers of an original screenplay ranged from $62,642 to $117,602 during the 2010–11 segment of the contract. The U.S. Department of Labor reports that writers employed in the movie industry had mean annual earnings of $78,680 in 2010.

Outlook

It will be hard to land a job as a screenwriter, especially in film and television, because so many people are attracted to the field. In this industry, it is helpful to network and make contacts. If you want to be a movie screenwriter, it is important to

The Oscar Goes To...

The following screenwriters were Oscar winners for best original screenplay:

2010: David Seidler, *The King's Speech*

2009: Mark Boal, *The Hurt Locker*

2008: Dustin Lance Black, *Milk*

2007: Diablo Cody, *Juno*

2006: Michael Arndt, *Little Miss Sunshine*

2005: Paul Haggis and Bobby Moresco, *Crash*

2004: Charlie Kaufman, *Eternal Sunshine of the Spotless Mind*

2003: Sofia Coppola, *Lost in Translation*

2002: Pedro Almodóvar, *Talk to Her*

2001: Julian Fellowes, *Gosford Park*

2000: Cameron Crowe, *Almost Famous*

For more information on Academy Award-winning films, visit http://www.oscars.org/awardsdatabase.

FOR MORE INFO

To learn more about the film industry, to read interviews and articles by noted screenwriters, and to find links to many other screenwriting-related sites on the Internet, visit the WGA Web site.

Writers Guild of America (WGA)
East Chapter
250 Hudson Street
New York, NY 10013-1413

212-767-7800
http://www.wgaeast.org

Writers Guild of America (WGA)
West Chapter
7000 West Third Street
Los Angeles, CA 90048-4329
800-548-4532
http://www.wga.org

work hard to break into the field and never stop following your dreams. On the brighter side, the growth of the cable industry has increased demand for original screenplays and adaptations. Additionally, people in foreign countries are increasingly interested in watching American movies. These developments should create more demand for screenwriters.

If you are thinking about becoming a screenwriter, you should also be open to careers in technical writing, journalism, or copywriting. Earning a college degree in a related field may help you find another job in case you have trouble breaking into the field.

Special and Visual Effects Technicians

What Special and Visual Effects Technicians Do

Special and visual effects technicians make fantastic things seem real in movies, theater, and television. They can make a spaceship fly to distant planets; create a three-headed, eight-armed green alien; or bring dinosaurs to life on the screen. There are two different types of effects technicians: special effects technicians and visual effects technicians. Both use special effects to wow viewers, but they use different methods to go about creating these effects.

Special effects technicians create actual physical effects that are shot while the camera is rolling during a scene. There are three main subspecialties in the field: makeup, pyrotechnics, and mechanical effects. *Makeup effects specialists* create masks and costumes. They build prosthetic devices, such as fake human or animal heads or limbs. They must be skilled at modeling, sewing, applying makeup, and mixing dyes. *Pyrotechnics effects specialists* are experts with firearms and explosives. They create explosions for dramatic scenes. This work can be very dangerous. Most states require them to be licensed in order to handle and set off explosives. *Mechanical effects specialists* build sets, props, and backgrounds. They build, install, and operate equipment mechanically or electrically. They usually are skilled in carpentry, electricity, welding, and robotics.

EXPLORING

- Read books about special effects. Following are a few suggestions: *Movie Special Effects*, by Liz Miles (Heinemann-Raintree, 2009); *Movie Science: 40 Mind-Expanding, Reality-Bending, Starstruck Activities for Kids*, by Jim Wiese (Wiley, 2001); *So You Want to Work in Animation & Special Effects?*, by Torene Svitil (Enslow Publishers, 2007); and *100% Pure Fake: Gross Out Your Friends and Family with 25 Great Special Effects!*, by Lyn Thomas (Kids Can Press, 2009).
- Use computer animation software programs that allow you to create special effects.
- Visit your school, public library and bookstores, or check online to read more about special effects technology. Look for magazines such as *Cinefex* (http://www.cinefex.com), *Variety* (http://www.variety.com), and *Hollywood Reporter* (http://www.hollywoodreporter.com).
- If you have a video camera, experiment with special effects in filming and editing.
- Work on school drama productions as a stagehand, sound technician, or makeup artist. You will learn about set and prop design, and how to use tools and mechanical and electrical equipment.
- Ask a teacher or counselor to arrange an information interview with a special or visual effects technician.

Visual effects technicians use computer software programs to add or improve effects after a film is made. These effects would be impossible or too costly to build. Visual effects technicians make it possible for a human face to change or "morph" into an animal's face, or for a realistic-looking bear to drink a popular soda. They typically work in an office or animation studio, separate from the actual filming location. Visual effects technicians also work in the computer and video game industry.

Education and Training

To be a special effects technician, you need to know about science and art. Take high school classes in art, sculpture, art history, chemistry, physics, shop, and computers. If you want to work as a visual effects technician, you should take as many computer science classes as possible, especially those that focus on animation and related topics.

Some universities have film and television programs that offer courses in special and visual effects. Visual effects technicians can also earn degrees in animation or computer and video game design. Most technicians in the industry say that the best way into this career is through experience working on a film crew.

Earnings

The U.S. Department of Labor (DOL) does not offer salary information for special effects technicians. It does report that average annual earnings of all wage and salary workers

Tips for Success

To be a successful special effects technician, you should

- have basic mechanical ability
- have good artistic skills
- be able to meet deadlines
- have good people skills
- be especially attentive to safety on the set
- be able to work long hours in varied environments
- be able to deal with stress

The Most Influential Visual Effects Films of All Time

1. *Star Wars* (1977)
2. *Blade Runner* (1982)
3. *2001: A Space Odyssey* (1968)
4. *The Matrix* (1999)
5. *Jurassic Park* (1993)
6. *Tron* (1982)
7. *King Kong* (1933)
8. *Close Encounters of the Third Kind* (1977)
9. *Alien* (1979)
10. *The Abyss* (1989)

Source: Visual Effects Society

in the motion picture and video industries were $32,604 in 2008.

The DOL classifies visual effects technicians under the heading of "multimedia artist and animator." Workers in these specialties who were employed in the motion picture and video industries earned annual mean salaries of $72,380 in 2010, according to the DOL. Salaries for all multimedia artists and animators ranged from less than $34,000 to more than $99,000. Technicians at some of the top effects houses can earn hundreds of thousands of dollars.

Outlook

The competition for jobs at film special and visual effects houses is very strong. For decades now, films and television shows of all kinds have used high-tech effects. This has inspired a whole generation of young people to enter the field.

Many people want to work in special and visual effects. Only very talented people with specialized training and knowledge of the latest technology will be able to land a job in this exciting, highly creative field.

FOR MORE INFO

For information about animated films and digital effects, visit the AWN Web site. At the site, you will find feature articles, a list of schools, and a career section.
Animation World Network (AWN)
6525 Sunset Boulevard, Garden Suite 10
Hollywood, CA 90028-7212
323-606-4200
info@awn.com
http://www.awn.com

The guild represents the interests of animation professionals in California. Visit its Web site for information on training, earnings, and the animation industry.
Animators Guild Local 839
1105 North Hollywood Way
Burbank, CA 91505-2528
818-845-7500
http://animationguild.org

For industry information, contact
Entertainment Software Association
575 7th Street, NW, Suite 300
Washington, DC 20004-1611
esa@theesa.com
http://www.theesa.com

For membership information, contact
International Animated Film Society-ASIFA Hollywood
2114 West Burbank Boulevard
Burbank, CA 91506-1232
818-842-4691
info@asifa-hollywood.org
http://www.asifa-hollywood.org

Visit the society's Web site for information about festivals and presentations and news about the industry.
Visual Effects Society
5535 Balboa Boulevard, Suite 205
Encino, CA 91316-1544
818-981-7861
info@visualeffectssociety.com
http://www.visualeffectssociety.com

This nonprofit organization represents the professional interests of women (and men) in animation. Visit its Web site for industry information, links to animation blogs, details on membership for high school students, and its quarterly newsletter.
Women in Animation
wia@womeninanimation.org
http://wia.animationblogspot.com

Stunt Performers

What Stunt Performers Do

Stunt performers work on film and television scenes that are risky and dangerous. They act out car crashes and chases. They participate in mock fist and sword fights. They actually fall from cars, motorcycles, horses, and buildings. They perform airplane and helicopter gags, ride through raging river rapids, and face wild animals, such as bulls, bears, and buffaloes. Some stunt performers focus on just one type of stunt.

There are two general types of stunt roles: *double* and *nondescript.* The first requires a stunt performer to double, or take the place of, a star actor in a dangerous scene. As a double, the stunt performer must portray the character in the same way as the star actor.

In a nondescript role, the stunt performer does not stand in for another actor, but plays an incidental character in a dangerous scene. An example of a nondescript role is a driver in a freeway chase scene. Stunt performers occasionally have speaking parts.

The idea for a stunt usually begins with the *screenwriter,* the person who writes the script for the movie or TV show. Once the stunts are written into the script, it is the job of the *director* (who oversees the entire film or TV show) to decide how they will appear on the screen. Directors, especially of large, action-filled movies, often seek the help of a *stunt coordinator.* A stunt coordinator can quickly decide if a stunt is possible and what is the best and safest way to perform it. Stunt coordinators plan

EXPLORING

- Read books about the work of stunt performers. Following are two suggestions: *Movie Stunts and Special Effects,* by Geoffrey M. Horn (Gareth Stevens Publishing, 2006) and *Stage Combat: Fisticuffs, Stunts, and Swordplay for Theater and Film,* by Jenn Boughn (Allworth Press, 2006).
- Stunt performers must be in top physical shape and train like athletes. To develop your physical strength and coordination, play on sports teams and participate in school athletics.
- Acting in school or church plays can teach you about taking direction.
- Theme parks and circuses use stunt performers. Visit these places and try to meet the performers after shows.
- Talk to a stunt performer about his or her career.

the stunt. They also oversee the setup and construction of special sets and materials and either hire or recommend the most qualified stunt performer.

Although a stunt may last only a few seconds in a movie, it can take several hours or even days to prepare for the stunt. Stunt performers work with props, makeup, wardrobe, and set design departments. They also work closely with the special and visual effects team. A carefully planned stunt can often be completed in just one take. It is more common for the stunt person to perform the stunt several times until the director is happy with the performance.

Stunt work can be very dangerous. Stunt performers do many things to make sure that they are safe during filming.

Stunt performers must have nerves of steel because they often perform dangerous stunts. (Butch McCartney, AP Photo/*Wausau Daily Herald*)

They use air bags, body pads, or cables in stunts involving falls or crashes. If a stunt performer must enter a burning building, he or she wears special fireproof clothing and protective skin cream.

Education and Training

No standard training exists for stunt performers. They usually start out by contacting stunt coordinators and asking for work. If the stunt coordinator thinks the person has the proper credentials, he or she will be hired for basic stunt work like fight scenes. A number of stunt schools, such as the United Stuntmen's Association International Stunt School, offer training to people who want to become stunt performers.

Tips for Success

To be a successful stunt performer, you should

- be in excellent physical shape
- be able to follow instructions
- have confidence in your abilities
- have self-discipline
- have good coordination
- be calm under pressure

Stunt performers get a lot of training on the job. Every new type of stunt has its own challenges. By working closely with stunt coordinators, performers learn how to eliminate most of the risks involved in stunts. Even so, injuries are very common among stunt performers. There is even the possibility of death during very dangerous stunts.

Earnings

Stunt performers earn the same day rate as other actors, plus extra pay for more difficult and dangerous stunts. Stunt performers must belong to the actor's union, the Screen Actors Guild (SAG). The SAG minimum day rate for stunt performers was $809 in 2010. Though this may seem like a lot of money, few stunt performers work every day. According to the SAG, the majority of its members make less than $7,500. But those who are in high demand can receive salaries of well over $100,000 a year.

Stunt Specialties

Following are some of the skills stunt performers learn in training programs at The United Stuntmen's Association:

- Climbing and rappelling
- Fire burns
- Foot falls

- High falls
- Horse work
- Martial arts
- Precision driving
- Special effects
- Stair falls
- Unarmed combat
- Weaponry

FOR MORE INFO

For more information on earnings and union membership, contact
Screen Actors Guild
5757 Wilshire Boulevard, 7th Floor
Los Angeles, CA 90036-3600
323-954-1600
http://www.sag.org

For information on opportunities in the industry, contact the following organizations:
Stuntmen's Association of Motion Pictures
5200 Lankershim Boulevard, Suite 190
North Hollywood, CA 91601-3100
818-766-4334
hq@stuntmen.com
http://www.stuntmen.com

Stuntwomen's Association of Motion Pictures
818-762-0907
http://www.stuntwomen.com

For information about the USA training program and images of stunt performers in action, visit the association's Web site.
United Stuntmen's Association (USA)
10924 Mukilteo Speedway, PMB 272
Mukilteo, WA 98275-5022
425-645-9552
iboushey@gmail.com
http://www.stuntschool.com

Outlook

There are more than 7,700 stunt performers who belong to the SAG, but only a small number work full time. It's difficult for new stunt performers to break into the business. The future of this career may be affected by computer technology. Moviemakers today use special effects and computer-generated imagery for action sequences. Computer-generated stunts are also safer. Safety on film sets has always been a major concern since many stunts are very dangerous. However, using live stunt performers can make a scene seem more real, so talented stunt performers will always be in demand.

Talent Agents and Scouts

What Talent Agents and Scouts Do

An agent is a salesperson who sells artistic talent. *Talent agents* represent actors, directors, writers, models, and other people who work in movies, television, and theater. They promote their talent and manage legal contracts and other business. Talent agents look for clients who have potential for success. Then they work very hard to promote their clients to film and television directors, casting directors, production companies, and other potential employers.

Agents find clients in several ways. They review portfolios, screen tests, and audiotapes to evaluate potential clients' appearance, voice, personality, experience, ability to take direction, and other factors. Agents who work for a talent agency might be assigned a client by the agency, based on experience or a like personality. Some agents also work as *talent scouts*. These workers actively search for new clients,

EXPLORING

- Watch current movies to get a sense of the established and up-and-coming talents in the film industry. Trace the careers of actors you like, including their early work in independent films, commercials, and stage work.
- Contact a local talent agent to learn more about the career.
- Volunteer or intern at a talent agency to find out more about the career.

whom they then bring to an agency. Or the clients themselves might approach agents who have good reputations and request their representation.

When an agent agrees to represent a client, they both sign a contract that specifies the extent of representation (what duties the agent will have), the time period the contract will last, payment, and other legal considerations.

Agents also work closely with the potential employers of their clients. They need to satisfy the needs of both parties. Agents who represent actors have a network of directors, producers, advertising executives, and photographers that they contact frequently to see if any of their clients can meet their needs.

When agents see a possible match between employer and client, they speak to both and quickly organize meetings, interviews, or auditions so that employers can meet potential hires and evaluate their work and capabilities. Agents must be persistent and aggressive on behalf of their clients. They spend time on the phone with employers, convincing them of their clients' talents and persuading them to hire clients.

When an employer agrees to hire a client, the agent helps negotiate a contract that outlines salary, benefits, promotional appearances, and other fees, rights, and obligations. Agents have to look out for the best interests of their clients and at the

Tips for Success

To be a successful talent agent or scout, you should

- be a good judge of talent
- have strong negotiation skills
- be hard working and aggressive
- be detail-oriented
- have good business sense
- be self-motivated
- have ambition
- have great communication skills

Words to Learn

audition in the movie industry, the process in which an actor meets with casting agents, directors, and other film professionals to demonstrate his or her qualifications for a role; during the audition, the actor may participate in a screen test

casting placing actors in roles for a film

contract a legal agreement between two parties

negotiation an oral or written process in which two parties

communicate to try to come to an agreement regarding salary, work duties, etc.

portfolio samples of an actor's or other film professional's work

screen tests scenes that are recorded on film

script a written overview of everything that happens in a movie, including dialogue, video and audio instructions, and the movements of the actors

same time satisfy employers in order to establish continuing, long-lasting relationships.

The largest talent agencies are located in Los Angeles and New York City, where the film industry is centered. Independent agents have offices throughout the country.

Education and Training

You should take courses in business, math, and accounting to prepare for the management aspects of an agent's job. Take English and speech courses to help develop good communication skills because you will need to be a good negotiator. You also need a good eye for talent, so be sure to develop knowledge of film and related areas.

FOR MORE INFO

For industry news, contact
Association of Talent Agents
9255 Sunset Boulevard, Suite 930
Los Angeles, CA 90069-3317
310-274-0628
http://www.agentassociation.com

For general information on management careers in the performing arts, contact
North American Performing Arts Managers and Agents
459 Columbus Avenue, Suite 133
New York, NY 10024-5129

conal@napama.org
http://www.napama.org

Visit the SAG Web site for information about acting in films and for a list of talent agencies.
Screen Actors Guild (SAG)
5757 Wilshire Boulevard, 7th Floor
Los Angeles, CA 90036-3600
323-954-1600
http://www.sag.org

Although some agents receive their training on the job, a bachelor's degree is strongly recommended for work in this field. Advanced degrees in law and business are becoming increasingly popular since talent agents must write contracts according to legal regulations.

Earnings

Earnings for agents vary greatly, depending on the success of the agent and his or her clients. An agency receives 10 to 15 percent of a client's fee for a project. An agent is then paid a commission by the agency as well as a base salary.

Talent agents in the movie industry earned mean salaries of $96,120 in 2010, according to the U.S. Department of Labor. Salaries for all agents ranged from less than $26,000 to $166,400. Top agents can earn more than $1 million a year.

Outlook

Although the number of people watching movies has increased greatly in recent years, competition for positions as talent agents and scouts is very intense. It may take years and years to become successful in the field. Some aspiring agents never make it in the business. On the plus side, overseas markets for U.S. films are expanding, so even films that don't do so well domestically (in the United States) can still turn a tidy profit. Also, more original cable television programming will lead to more actors and performers seeking to hire agents. These expanding markets should create steady opportunities for the most experienced talent agents and scouts.

Glossary

accredited   approved as meeting established standards for providing good training and education; this approval is usually given by an independent organization of professionals

annual salary   the money an individual earns for an entire year of work

apprentice   a person who is learning a trade by working under the supervision of a skilled worker; apprentices often receive classroom instruction in addition to their supervised practical experience

associate's degree   an academic rank or title granted by a community or junior college or similar institution to graduates of a two-year program of education beyond high school

bachelor's degree   an academic rank or title given to a person who has completed a four-year program of study at a college or university; also called an undergraduate degree or baccalaureate

bonus   an award of money in addition to one's typical salary that is given to an employee for extra-special work or achievement on the job

career   an occupation for which a worker receives training and has an opportunity for advancement

certified   approved as meeting established requirements for skill, knowledge, and experience in a particular field; people are certified by an organization of professionals in their field

college   a higher education institution that is above the high school level

community college   a public or private two-year college attended by students who do not usually live at the college; graduates of a community college receive an associate's degree and may transfer to a four-year college or university to complete a bachelor's degree

diploma   a certificate or document given by a school to show that a person has completed a course or has graduated from the school

distance education   a type of educational program that allows students to take classes and complete their education by mail or the Internet

doctorate   the highest academic rank or title granted by a graduate school to a person who has completed a two- to three-year program after having received a master's degree

fellowship   a financial award given for research projects or dissertation assistance; fellowships are commonly offered at the graduate, postgraduate, or doctoral levels

freelancer   a worker who is not a regular employee of a company; they work for themselves and do not receive a regular paycheck

fringe benefit   a payment or benefit to an employee in addition to regular wages or salary; examples of fringe benefits include a pension, a paid vacation, and health or life insurance

graduate school   a school that people may attend after they have received their bachelor's degree; people who complete an educational program at a graduate school earn a master's degree or a doctorate

intern   an advanced student (usually one with at least some college training) in a professional field who is employed in a job that is intended to provide supervised practical experience for the student

internship   1. the position or job of an intern; 2. the period of time when a person is an intern

junior college   a two-year college that offers courses like those in the first half of a four-year college program; graduates of a junior college usually receive an associate's degree and may transfer to a four-year college or university to complete a bachelor's degree

liberal arts   the subjects covered by college courses that develop broad general knowledge rather than specific occupational skills; the liberal arts are often considered to include philosophy, literature and the arts, history, language, and some courses in the social sciences and natural sciences

major (in college)   the academic field in which a student specializes and receives a degree

master's degree   an academic rank or title granted by a graduate school to a person who has completed a one- or two-year program after having received a bachelor's degree

pension   an amount of money paid regularly by an employer to a former employee after he or she retires from working

scholarship   A gift of money to a student to help the student pay for further education

social studies   courses of study (such as civics, geography, and history) that deal with how human societies work

starting salary   salary paid to a newly hired employee; the starting salary is usually a smaller amount than is paid to a more experienced worker

technical college   a private or public college offering two- or four-year programs in technical subjects; technical colleges offer courses in both general and technical subjects and award associate's degrees and bachelor's degrees

undergraduate   a student at a college or university who has not yet received a degree

undergraduate degree   see bachelor's degree

union   an organization whose members are workers in a particular industry or company; the union works to gain better wages, benefits, and working conditions for its members; also called a labor union or trade union

vocational school   a public or private school that offers training in one or more skills or trades

wage   money that is paid in return for work done, especially money paid on the basis of the number of hours or days worked

Browse and Learn More

Books

Albert, Lisa Rondinelli. *So You Want to Be a Film or TV Actor?* Berkeley Heights, N.J.: Enslow Publishers, 2008.

Boughn, Jenn. *Stage Combat: Fisticuffs, Stunts, and Swordplay for Theater and Film.* New York: Allworth Press, 2006.

Buckley, Annie. *Making Movies.* Mankato, Minn.: The Child's World, 2006.

———. *Movies.* Ann Arbor, Mich.: Cherry Lake Publishing, 2008.

Cohn, Jessica. *Animator.* New York: Gareth Stevens Publishing, 2009.

Desjardins, Christian, and Christopher Young. *Inside Film Music: Composers Speak.* Los Angeles: Silman-James Press, 2007.

Dunkleberger, Amy. *So You Want to Be a Film or TV Director?* Berkeley Heights, N.J.: Enslow Publishers, 2007.

———. *So You Want to Be a Film or TV Editor?* Berkeley Heights, N.J.: Enslow Publishers, 2007.

———. *So You Want to Be a Film or TV Screenwriter?* Berkeley Heights, N.J.: Enslow Publishers, 2007.

Dunn, Mary R. *I Want to Make Movies.* New York: PowerKids Press, 2008.

Franks, Katie. *I Want to Be a Movie Star.* New York: PowerKids Press, 2007.

Grabham, Tim, Suridh Hassan, Dave Reeve, and Clare Richards. *Movie Maker: The Ultimate Guide to Making Films.* Somerville, Mass.: Candlewick Press, 2010.

Hamlett, Christina. *Screenwriting for Teens: The 100 Principles of Screenwriting Every Budding Writer Must Know.* Studio City, Calif.: Michael Wiese Productions, 2006.

Horn, Geoffrey M. *Movie Acting.* New York: Gareth Stevens Publishing, 2006.

———. *Movie Animation.* New York: Gareth Stevens Publishing, 2006.

———. *Movie Soundtracks and Sound Effects.* New York: Gareth Stevens Publishing, 2006.

———. *Movie Stunts and Special Effects.* New York: Gareth Stevens Publishing, 2006.

———. *Writing, Producing, and Directing Movies.* New York: Gareth Stevens Publishing, 2006.

Lanier, Troy, and Clay Nichols. *Filmmaking for Teens: Pulling Off Your Shorts.* 2d ed. Studio City, Calif.: Michael Wiese Productions, 2010.

Marcovitz, Hal. *Computer Animation.* Farmington Hills, Mich.: Lucent Books, 2008.

Mayfield, Katherine. *Acting A to Z: The Young Person's Guide to a Stage or Screen Career.* New York: Back Stage Books, 2007.

Miles, Liz. *Movie Special Effects.* Chicago: Heinemann-Raintree, 2009.

O'Brien, Lisa, and Stephen MacEachern. *Lights, Camera, Action!: Making Movies and TV from the Inside Out.* Toronto, ON. Canada: Maple Tree Press, 2007.

O'Neill, Joseph. *Movie Director.* Ann Arbor, Mich.: Cherry Lake Publishing, 2009.

Stoller, Bryan Michael. *Filmmaking for Dummies.* 2d ed. New York: For Dummies, 2008.

Svitil, Torene. *So You Want to Work in Animation & Special Effects?* Berkeley Heights, N.J.: Enslow Publishers, 2007.

Svitil, Torene, and Amy Dunkleberger. *So You Want to Work in Set Design, Costuming, or Make-up?* Berkeley Heights, N.J.: Enslow Publishers, 2008.

Thomas, Lyn. *100% Pure Fake: Gross Out Your Friends and Family with 25 Great Special Effects!* Tonawanda, N.Y.: Kids Can Press, 2009.

Wiese, Jim. *Movie Science: 40 Mind-Expanding, Reality-Bending, Starstruck Activities for Kids.* Hoboken, N.J.: Wiley, 2001.

Periodicals

American Cinematographer
http://www.theasc.com

Animation Magazine
http://www.animationmagazine.net

Animation World Magazine
http://www.awn.com/magazines/animation-world-magazine

The Artisan
http://www.local706.org/artisan.cfm

Cinefex
http://www.cinefex.com

Creative Kids
http://www.prufrock.com/client/client_pages/prufrock_jm_createkids.cfm

Hollywood Reporter
http://www.hollywoodreporter.com

Screen Actor
http://www.sag.org/screenactor

Time for Kids
http://www.timeforkids.com/TFK

Variety
http://www.variety.com

Web Sites

Academy of Motion Picture Arts and Sciences
http://www.oscars.org

Acting Workshop On-Line: So You Want to Be an Actor

http://www.redbirdstudio.com/AWOL/acting2.html

AMC Filmsite

http://www.filmsite.org

American Film Institute

http://www.afi.com

American Library Association: Great Web Sites for Kids

http://www.ala.org/greatsites

AnimationMentor.com

http://animationmentor.com

Animation World Network

http://www.awn.com

The Big Cartoon Database

http://www.bcdb.com

Box Office Mojo

http://www.boxofficemojo.com

Cartoonster

http://www.kidzdom.com/tutorials

Chuck Jones

http://www.chuckjones.com

The Internet Movie Database

http://www.imdb.com

Pixar

http://www.pixar.com

The Walt Disney Family Museum

http://disney.go.com/disneyatoz/familymuseum

Index